Praise for *Nice Try*

"*Nice Try* makes me wish I was friends with Josh in high school. His take on the world is something we need more of—it's optimistic, observant, sincere, and insanely funny. Read this book."

—Hasan Minaj, host of *Patriot Act with Hasan Minaj*

"Josh Gondelman is a comedian who looks like an author, so this book makes a lot of sense. Like him, it's hilarious, excellent, and fun."

—Pete Holmes, author of *Comedy Sex God*

"Josh Gondelman reinforces what I love so deeply about his writing: chock full of wit, so wonderfully hilarious, and unafraid to be vulnerable and honest. Yes, he is known as one of the nicest dudes in comedy, but he's also one of the most funny and consistent. This book will not disappoint, so stop reading this blurb already and read the book!"

—Phoebe Robinson, author of
Everything's Trash, But It's Okay

"Reading *Nice Try* is like carrying around a good friend with you, someone who's funny and compassionate and always reminding you to do better. If you're lucky enough to read Josh Gondelman, you're sure to leave the experience a happier, kinder person. (And as a real bonus, you'll laugh, too.) There's good in the world yet—*Nice Try* is a great reminder of that."

—Scaachi Koul, author of *One Day We'll All
Be Dead and None of This Will Matter*

"Josh Gondelman is hilarious. This book proves he clearly wouldn't have survived if he wasn't."

—Judd Apatow, author of *Sick in the Head*

"Everyone in comedy knows Josh Gondelman is funny and nice, but he's better than nice, he's good. This collection of essays will make you laugh out loud and want to be a better human."

—Akilah Hughes, author of *Obviously*

"I laughed on every single page of Josh's book and insisted on reading much of it aloud to whomever was sitting next to me. I did not always know these people, but I choose to believe they loved it too."

—Jill Twiss, author of *A Day in the Life of Marlon Bundo*

"Like the best conversation with your smartest, funniest friend, these essays leave you feeling a little bit better about the world. Gondelman doesn't flinch from self-examination or the complexities of life, but navigates both with such warmth and wit that I miss his company already."

—Cynthia D'Aprix Sweeney, author of *The Nest*

"Gondelman's chops as a comedy writer are on full display throughout, and his observations are hilariously spot-on. . . . [His] fun, witty book is a marvel of emotional depth and cutting one-liners."

—*Publishers Weekly*

Nice Try

Nice Try

STORIES OF BEST INTENTIONS AND MIXED RESULTS

Josh Gondelman

HARPER ● PERENNIAL

NEW YORK ● LONDON ● TORONTO ● SYDNEY ● NEW DELHI ● AUCKLAND

HARPER ● PERENNIAL

HarperCollins books may be purchased for educational, business, or sales promotional use. For information, please email the Special Markets Department at SPsales@harpercollins.com.

FIRST EDITION

Designed by Jen Overstreet

Library of Congress Cataloging-in-Publication Data

Names: Gondelman, Josh, 1985- author.
Title: Nice try : stories of best intentions and mixed results / Josh Gondelman.
Description: First edition. | New York : HarperCollinsPublishers, [2019] | HarperPerennial paperback. | Includes bibliographical references and index. | Summary: "Emmy-Award winning writer and comedian Josh Gondelman's collection of personal stories of best intentions and mixed results"— Provided by publisher.
Identifiers: LCCN 2019021584 | ISBN 9780062852755 (hardcover)
Subjects: LCSH: Life skills—Humor. | Success—Humor. | Maturation (Psychology)—Humor. | Gondelman, Josh, 1985—Humor.
Classification: LCC PN6231.L49 G66 2019 | DDC 818/.602—dc23
LC record available at https://lccn.loc.gov/2019021584

ISBN 978-0-06-285275-5

19 20 21 22 23 LSC 10 9 8 7 6 5 4 3 2 1

To Maris, in hopes that having a book dedicated
to her will make her enemies jealous

I want you to be nice until it's time to not be nice.
—Dalton, *Road House*

Contents

Introduction   xiii

If at First You Don't Succeed . . .

Nice Guys Finish Dessert Last   3

Just Give Me a Minute   10

A Few of My Greatest Fears,
in No Particular Order   22

1-800-GOOD-PORN   24

A Technicality   29

You Don't Know, Now You Know   30

Things That Make Me Feel Grown-Up
(in Order of Increasing Adulthood)   47

A Worthy Adversary   48

The Present-Tense Conjugation of the
Spanish Verb *Nadar*, Which Means "to Swim"   60

Screech   61

I Hope These Years Aren't the
Best of Your Lives   68

It Was Funny at the Time   74

Don't Aim, Just Throw   76

. . . Try, Try Again

Weathering the Tantrums   91

The Thanksgiving Dragon   103

Some Things That I, a Childcare
Professional, Was Professionally Obligated
to Say to Kids   108

Good Deeds, Unrewarded   109

Have Fun   116

The Blank Postcard   123

Things I Have Tried (with Varying Degrees
of Success) at the Behest of Women I Was
Dating at the Time or to Whom I Am Married   142

Good Will Hunting Isn't Science Fiction   143

Sorry, Not Sorry   145

Gap Years   154

Third Time's a Charm?

The Three True Stories of How We Met   163

Fish Tacos   176

Tickle Me Fancy   179

A Good Game   185

The Unsung Virtue of Telling People What
They Want to Hear   198

An Element of Style   207

Bizzy   212

A Partial List of Names I Call My Dog,
Whose Real Name Is Bizzy   229

"I Also Do Michael Jackson"   231

The Best Moments of My Wedding #3–10   240

Don't Let the Bastards Grind You Down   242

Acknowledgments   **251**

Introduction

Before I left for college, my dad sat me down on the living room couch and gave me some advice.

"When you go away to school, I want you to remember—" He paused, leaving me enough time to wonder exactly what kind of wisdom he was about to bestow on me. My dad is not prone to grand proclamations, and he also wasn't a big fan of his own college experience. "I want you to remember," he continued, "when you leave for college, don't bring dirty clothes with you. You'll have to do laundry right away, and you'll go through all your change. Here, I want you to have this."

My father then got up from his chair, reached into his pocket, and pulled out an orange pill bottle, which felt like a hard turn for the conversation to take. Had my dad been dealing Adderall on the side, like a low-stakes *Breaking Bad*? He dropped the bottle into my hand, and it landed with an unexpected heft and a jingle. It was full of quarters. He sat back down, waited another beat, and continued his heart-to-heart in a way that felt less thoroughly prepped. At the very least, he hadn't brought any props for the second part of the talk.

"I think you're going to do really well in college," he said, and then he paused again, as if considering whether to say the next part out loud or keep it to himself. "You know, when you started high school, I never told you this, but I was worried you'd be too nice and people would take advantage of you. I'm really glad that didn't happen."

If I'm being honest, I have to admit that I gave him good reason to fear for my safety and social well-being as I entered ninth grade. I'd always had a wet paint personality, bright and shiny and vulnerable to the elements. I was proud that he trusted me to go off into the world, or at least as far as Brandeis University.

"Thanks," I said.

"You're welcome."

We hugged, and he left the room, and I sat there with my medicine bottle full of quarters, most of which I probably ended up lending to someone who never paid me back.

Years later, people still got the same impression of me.

"Have you met Gondelman?" my friend Andy said to his friend Dave at a party when I was twenty-five. "He's super nice."

Dave's face fell.

"No, but he's funny, too," Andy reassured him.

My reputation often precedes me in social and professional circles, and not always in positive ways. For a comedian, "nice" can be shorthand for someone's work being bland. And on a personal level, "nice" is about as meaningful as saying someone "has decent breath" or "is usually punctual."

But, still, where I'm known at all, I'm known as a nice guy, which I think I am. But I'm trying to be other things, too, even though sometimes I'm not great at that. After all, it's *nice* to waste eighty dollars trying to win your date a stuffed animal on the Coney Island boardwalk. But it's certainly not financially responsible. And when you lose the carnival game, and the carny[1] feels bad and gives you the prize anyway, it's a little undignified, and you'll wish you'd set firmer boundaries. This is not a hypothetical example.

There's a scene from the movie *Road House* that I think about a lot. I mean, there are a lot of scenes from that movie that play often in my mind: the ones where Patrick Swayze rips out a guy's throat, the one where Ben Gazzara's character watches smugly as a monster truck drives over all the cars at a dealership owned by his enemy, the one where after receiving stitches from a doctor who asks if he enjoys pain Swayze responds, stoically, "Pain don't hurt." *Road House* is either one of the best terrible movies ever made or the worst good movie ever made.

But there is one scene in particular I look to more than the others. Patrick Swayze (in the movie, he's called "Dalton," but come on . . . it's Patrick Swayze) has just taken over as head of security at the Double Deuce, a Kansas City dive bar where patrons throw bottles at the live band and employees have (uncomfortably explicit, if you're watching with your dad) sex with each other on their fifteen-minute breaks. Swayze/Dalton is outlining his new guidelines for the bar's bouncers. The final tenet of his code is both simple and unexpected to the team of fistbrains working the door.

---

1   Do we still say "carny"?

"Be nice," he advises them. And when the staff questions him, he elaborates. "If somebody gets in your face and calls you a cock-sucker, I want you to be nice. Ask him to walk. Be nice. If he won't walk, walk him, but be nice. If you can't walk him, one of the others will help you, and you will both be nice."

Then there's a little back-and-forth between Dalton/Swayze and his employees regarding contingencies such as "What if he calls my mama a whore?" It's not important for our purposes here. What's important is how Swayzeton concludes his speech:

"I want you to be nice until it's time to not be nice."

"So, uh, how are we supposed to know when that is?" says a large, violent employee with the IQ of chewed gum.

"You won't," says Patrick Swayze. "I'll let you know."

That last part always feels like such a relief to me. How great would it be to have someone in your life to tell you when to flip the switch from Nice to Badass; or, in my case, from Nice to Irri-table? Because not every problem can be solved by nice-ing your way through it. And being Not Nice doesn't always imply being Mean. It could mean being Firm or Uncompromising or Indig-nant or Guarded or Assertive (all of which I am historically bad at being).

And I'm not saying the right thing to do is to be, in all circum-stances, Not Nice. That is an occasionally effective strategy that doesn't scale. There's no valor in being a person who "tells it like it is" if you use that as a license to tell it mean and racist. Some-times you are still working under the umbrella of Nice, but just being polite and agreeable isn't enough. It's much better in many cases to be Generous or Righteous or Considerate or Forgiving or

Understanding. You can't do any of those things without being nice, but you sure as hell can be nice without doing that stuff, too.

All of this has been confusing to me, as a former Nice Boy who is trying to be a Good Guy. Because that means by turns being nice, and being kind of a dick if the situation calls for it. And then sometimes you have to be assertive. And other times it's about taking a loss so someone you love can win, and weathering hard times while staying tender. And then sometimes being a good person means doing drugs in a bathroom stall in a bowling alley. And other times it means accepting a trophy for a film you didn't make that was entered into a festival it had no business being in. At least, I think that's what it means.

If at First
You Don't
Succeed . . .

Nice Guys Finish Dessert Last

During my wife's wedding vows, in front of all the friends and family that could fit in the room (plus the DJ/Michael Jackson impersonator we'd inadvertently hired), she told me that I wasn't nice. It wasn't something I was used to hearing. Sure, strangers on the internet had called me an idiot. And women I'd dated in the past had, as things were deteriorating, told me I was inconsiderate or selfish or distracted. But the problem was never that I wasn't *nice*. On at least one occasion in my early to midtwenties, I was told I was "too nice," which is a very sweet euphemism meaning "simply not a person I am interested in having sex with in the foreseeable future." Which is, you know, fair.

So when Maris, which is my wife's name (sorry I didn't mention that before), said on the day of our wedding that I was "not nice," it really felt like she saw something in me that no one had ever noticed before. And I almost cried in a good way, but the tears stayed inside until midway through the reception when the DJ stepped out from behind his equipment in a red leather jacket and a silver rhinestone glove, and I laughed so hard I couldn't hold them back anymore.

Although, not to contradict my wife, but I am actually very nice. I think it's probably genetic.

There's a Gondelman family legend about my grandfather that explains pretty much my whole personality. None of my living family members were present for these events, so a few of the details might be inaccurate, but the emotional center of this story reverberates in my bones to this day.

Decades ago, my dad's parents were invited to a dinner party. I imagine that it being a social gathering in the 1950s, it consisted of a lot of smoking indoors, and all the men were wearing full suits for some reason. One guy probably played "God Bless America" on a piano while his wife sang, and then everyone saluted. I am, of course, extrapolating this from *Mad Men* episodes I sort of remember.

When dessert came out, the evening took a turn. The guests were presented with plates of homemade pastry. No one knew it at the time, but apparently the party's hostess had tasted a version of the dish served by a friend, and, smitten immediately, she had requested the recipe. The hostess's friend was reluctant to give the recipe away; it was a family secret. But she didn't want the hostess to know how petty she was. So, instead of outright refusing, she wrote down a version of the recipe *with an ingredient missing*. The hostess had no idea she'd been sabotaged, set up to fail by someone we would now call a "frenemy" but back then people referred to as "a real piece of work, if you know what I mean."

At the party where the booby-trapped dessert was served, no one took more than two bites. Each guest managed a single nibble and laid down their fork as if toppling their king to concede a chess match. Some held their napkins to their lips as if they were sharing secrets with them and spat out what they'd bitten off whole.

Not Morton Gondelman,[1] though. My grandfather, undeterred by the horrible taste of the food in front of him, dug in hard like he was burying a body in the woods. The other guests alternated staring and trying not to stare in horror as he cleaned his plate. Then, without flinching, he requested a second helping and devoured that, too.

"Papa," I said, on hearing this story for the first time (with the accent on the first syllable, not the second, the way a fancy European toddler calls for his father), "why did you ask for seconds?"

His response was immediate, as if he could imagine no other answer. "I didn't want her to feel bad."

Even as a child, I recognized this as a tremendous act of generosity. Sure, they say Jesus died for our sins, but did he ever choke down *two* slices of chocolate cake, dry as hairballs because the recipe deliberately excluded eggs, in a desperate effort to spare the feelings of just one person? I think not. Incidentally, there is no way that plan worked. Considering not a single other attendee got even halfway through the dessert, my grandfather's gambit undoubtedly came off less as "This food is delicious!" and more like "My taste buds were destroyed years ago in a horrible scalding-hot-pizza incident!"

By both nature and nurture, that is my heritage. Technically, I'm Jewish. I was bar mitzvahed, and I enjoy the ritualized eating

---

1 Yes, *the* Morton Gondelman, owner at the time of Morton's, the women's clothing boutique in downtown Boston.

of carbohydrates. But more than that, I was raised *nice*. I have a nice mom and a nice dad, and their niceness was instilled in me at a very young age. They're not just nice, they're *good*, too. My dad was active for years in his local chapter of the Painters and Allied Trades union, a vocal advocate for his colleagues. My mom was a devoted educator. My sister, Jenna, a pediatric physical therapist, is also both nice and good.

As a child, I was a nice boy, and when you're a kid, niceness is enough. Or at least, that's the feedback I got. You say please and thank you. You wait in line without wandering off. You refrain from punching other kids in the face, no matter how annoying they are. You follow directions. And if you do those things, you're a Good Kid, which is pretty much the highest level of being a kid other than Child Prodigy, which comes with way more baggage, and honestly, who needs that?

But niceness is only enough under the best possible conditions. It relies on having adults in your life looking out for you, and on not facing prejudice, even as a child, based on your race, gender, religion, economic background, physical and mental ability, or sexuality. But these are all thoughts I had as a grown-up, not as a kid.

So, let's say you're a Good Kid, and you ask people how they're doing when you see them, and you share your fruit snacks with your friends. Under ideal circumstances, that's all that anyone expects, and nobody asks much more of you. My parents instilled me with a habit of being respectful toward everyone I encountered, not to mention impeccable telephone manners that often got me mocked once everyone I knew had a cell phone.

"Hello, may I please speak to Eric?"

"Who the hell else would be answering my phone? It was literally in my pocket until you called."

And then you grow up, and everything's different. Being a Nice Kid is commendable. It's a credit to your parents, and it buys you a lot of goodwill with authority figures.

As an adult, I avoid self-identifying as a Nice Guy for two reasons. Reason number one is that "nice" is one of those things that when you tell someone you're it, it probably means you're the exact opposite. Like when someone says they are "super chill and low maintenance," it means scheduling lunch with them will take a full week of emails while they bend you to the will of their rigorous schedule and dietary preferences. Then, when you get something on the books, they will send you an online calendar invite, the type A person's reminder that they don't trust you to show up when you promised to show up. Similarly, when you say you are a nice person, it's often cover for sentiments like, "So if I scream in your face, please know that it is your fault and not something I, a nice person, would otherwise be doing."

Secondly, though, there's the issue of the capital N, capital G Nice Guy. The Nice Guy is always bemoaning how nobody respects him. More specifically, he's always upset that women won't date him. Women just don't want Nice Guys anymore, they lament. But, of course, underneath that refrain is a sense of entitlement for doing the bare minimum. "I held the door open for you! Isn't that enough?" Or, "I paid for dinner! What more do you want?" It's gross, and it's sexist, and it really fucks it up for everyone who takes pride in writing prompt, courteous thank-you emails and doesn't expect a hand job for it.

But those are small-time problems. The big issue with being nice as an ethos is that it's not a code that prepares you to solve every conflict you face in the adult world. Just saying please and thank you doesn't get you very far in a job interview. A handpicked bouquet of flowers won't solve systemic racism. Gentle, collaborative play is not helpful when your partner asks to be choked in bed. Being nice isn't just insufficient; it's sometimes the straight-up *wrong* thing to do.

Plus, when you're outwardly nice, people assume you're a pushover, which in my case is fair because I am one. But if you've got a cheerful, friendly demeanor, people act like you don't know better, like you've never heard of poverty or broken a bone. Optimists never get credit for the effort it takes to keep believing things are going to be okay. Here's a secret: most optimists know the world is full of horrors. They just think it can be improved. But especially in New York City, where I live, if you show a glimmer of hopefulness, everyone acts like you're a Disney princess who just woke up from a thousand-year slumber after a prince with a pure heart kissed your cold, cursed lips. And while we're on the topic, how come every fairy tale is about a prince saving a beleaguered damsel? Forget the problems with painting women as frail; are we really supposed to believe no one ever puts men in magically induced comas?

People especially love a guy who is *secretly nice*. There's no personality type people love more than a dude who's salty on the outside and sweet on the inside, like a gourmet caramel.

"That guy's kind of an asshole, huh?" you might say, in reference to a coworker who interrupted a conversation about the new season of your favorite TV show to say he couldn't get through the first episode because it was "too derivative" and that he "can't understand how anyone is obtuse enough to look past the lazy writing."

"Hey," your friend might say to you, in a hushed and reverent tone. "He's a little gruff, sure. But he once texted me after a breakup even though I didn't expect him to. He is a *hero*."

It's not entirely unfair. There are lots of ways to be a nice person while also being a terrible person. People politely screw each other over all the time. Even the Zodiac killer was polite enough to remember to leave a note after he did a murder.

There are also lots of things people do that aren't nice but in the long run reverberate with kindness and goodness. Telling someone he is about to leave the house dressed the way a toddler might style himself for his birthday party isn't exactly *pleasant*. But it is useful information that could save a loved one from seeing a photo tagged on Facebook and thinking, *How did it come to this?* (Although, granted, maybe there's a more gentle way to phrase that critique.) It's also mean to straight-up tell someone to fuck off, but when that person is a creep or a homophobe, it's good to be kind of a dickhead to them.

And there's a lot of stuff that "good kids" don't do that is totally fine for "good people." Talking back. Swearing. Drinking booze. Smoking pot. Having sex. Having *weird* sex. Getting mad. Getting dumped. Dumping someone else. All the parts of being a grown-up that Nice Kids can be warned off of.

Niceness, it turns out, is the floor for goodness, not the ceiling.

Just Give Me a Minute

The last time I almost fainted came at the most embarrassing moment possible. I had just started dating my now-wife Maris. I didn't know her well, but I did know that she worked in the publishing industry. So, as a fourth or fifth date, I invited her to see *Gone Girl* because it was a movie based on a book, which is a lot like a book. That was the only fact I knew about *Gone Girl* when we walked in.

It turns out that in the movie *Gone Girl*, Rosamund Pike plays Gone Girl, who marries Ben Affleck[1] before deciding she hates him, faking her own death, and framing him for it. Which, honestly, I get. This is a bad movie to see on a man-woman date because men are afraid of being framed for murder, and women

---

1 I think this qualifies as his best performance because you watch him playing a townie asshole and think, *Is he just . . . like that? Is that his real personality? I bet that's just what Ben Affleck does all day.* That to me is good acting, when you believe the character is just the actor's real personality.

are relieved to watch a movie where—surprise!—the lady's romantic partner *doesn't* actually kill her. The emotional experience of watching this movie, therefore, varies wildly depending on the viewer's gender.

But this is not a story about the plot of *Gone Girl*. It's a story about fainting, which requires just a little bit more explanation of the plot of *Gone Girl*.

In a scene near the end of the movie, Gone Girl frames Neil Patrick Harris, her wealthy nontownie ex-boyfriend, for assaulting her. (For the second time! Fool me once, *Gone Girl* . . .) Gone Girl, it turns out, is very good at framing people for things. But this time, instead of leaving Neil Patrick Harris to face the consequences of the justice system like she did with Ben Affleck, she murders him while they are having sex. And what a murder! She stabs him in the throat (one of the worst places to be stabbed, in my opinion) and leaves him to gurgle to death.

Either the sound designer of *Gone Girl* was incredible, or Neil Patrick Harris is even more talented than we thought, because his gurgling sounds exactly like someone drinking a smoothie made of ground beef through a straw. It turns out he's actually a quadruple threat! Acting! Singing! Dancing! Gurgling! The scene is very gross, grosser than anything else in the movie would lead you to believe was coming, like finding a human foot in your sock drawer. *Terrific,* I thought, as I felt myself go pale in the dark theater. *It's happening.*

"I'll be right back," I whispered to Maris, and I slipped out into the lobby of the movie theater. Then I slumped to the floor with my back against a column. I felt sick and must have looked sicker than that, because a concession salesperson cast me a long, suspicious glance as she walked past me to see if I was a drunk teenager about to puke on the carpet. I nodded, hoping to suggest that I was not an unruly teen, just a clammy, maladjusted adult. Nothing to see here.

I pulled out my phone to text Maris that I was grabbing some water and would be back in a minute. But, because I had a two-year-old iPhone, the battery had gone from full to zero percent while sitting unused in my pocket during the movie. *Okay,* I thought. *Just give it a few minutes and sneak back in. She'll assume you were doing something less embarrassing than this, like, I don't know, having diarrhea or walking into a parking meter while taking a selfie.*

Fortunately, I knew exactly what was going on with my body. Unfortunately, it's because it had happened too many times before.

The first time I fainted, I was eleven years old. I didn't know then that it was fainting. It's a word that I associated with Victorian baronesses having their blood drawn to have their humors examined. For years, I called it "passing out" or "needing a minute." But it was fainting. I fainted. I'm a fainter.

What was embarrassing as a child has only grown more shameful as an adult. Fainting represents a betrayal of your body against your will. It's like being unable to handle your liquor, but without the readily diagnosed intoxicant. To the outside observer, fainting is an effect without a visible cause.

Worst of all, though, to faint is to be vulnerable. There's the physical vulnerability, of course, the crashing to the ground like an imploding building. But the worst part is the pity—friends' and strangers' wide, sympathetic eyes. *You poor, delicate Fabergé egg of a person*, their faces communicate without a word. *You must possess a soul too gentle for this cruel and thorny world.* I picture myself as a detached intellect, governed by reason, cool under pressures both real and imagined, piloting my body smoothly and capably through the world. My history of infrequent but unavoidable fainting proves that definitively untrue. I am a man-size cavity, tender and susceptible to perceiving any tickling breeze as a hurricane-force wind. Or, in my experience, any description of something I find *too yucky*.

As a young know-it-all, I smugly read well above my grade level. Reading, I learned early on, serves dual purposes; it is fun to do *and* it lets you feel superior to other people. The best thing about books, though, was that I could read whichever ones I wanted. My parents, who kept a keen eye on my diet of television, movies, and video games, saw reading as a good unto itself.

My mom and my dad (but mostly my mom) had an extensive collection of literature, and I picked through it with one eye toward what was *good* and the other focused on what was *bad*. I tore through *The Catcher in the Rye* and *Lord of the Flies* in elementary school, my pretween brain vibrating with a mixture of titillation and pretension. *Ahh, so many swears. Very grown-up*, I would think. And, *Even on an island, I would know it is bad to murder a little boy with glasses, because I am a little boy with glasses.* Books hit the sweet spot of my personality; they let me experience something taboo and adult (or at the very least, young adult) without breaking any rules.

It was a book that first exposed my fragility to the world,

revealing just how sheltered I had been. My fifth-grade class took a trip to the local public library, where I checked out a copy of *Superstitious*, the young adult author R. L. Stine's first horror novel for . . . old adults. Like (roughly) every single child I knew, I was obsessed with Stine's Goosebumps series. It took only a few months for me to grow anesthetized to the shock of signature Goosebumps twists: ventriloquist dummies coming to life, Polaroid cameras foretelling doom for the subjects of their photographs, and summer camps full of more-terrifying monsters than the ones that populate most summer camps even.

So, as my classmates browsed the Hardy Boys and Baby-Sitters Club selections, I made my way into the adult fiction section of the Stoneham Public Library. The librarians didn't shepherd me back to my classmates, as I often browsed in search of a John Grisham book, because as a fifth grader I had the taste of a fifty-seven-year-old father of three.

The sensation of finding *Superstitious* was not unlike the feeling of coming across scrambled porn[2] on an obscure cable channel. When I held this book in my hands, I didn't know its exact contents, but I knew I'd come away changed having absorbed them. *Superstitious* had a hard spine, rather than the flimsy paper-

---

2 In the 1990s, before digital cable, an enterprising young person could turn to where the Spice channel would be if his parents paid for it and try to make out the sexual activity through the static. The project necessitated the vigilance of a sailor spotting nearby cliffs through a thick fog, and often bore paltry results. But when you caught a brief glimpse of flesh on flesh, it felt like a flicker of insight into the adult world.

back of a child's horror novel, which to me meant Serious Literature. The front cover bore the ominous image of a black cat with
glowing green eyes, a tasteful and mature symbol of the macabre.
No more moody, masked teens wielding knives, or lawn gnomes
come to life on the cover of my reading material, thank you very
much. Also, it had a lot of pages, which would make me look
impressive when I carried it around at school. On every level, *Superstitious* represented adult fiction. Reading it would signify my
intellectual, and more important, my emotional, maturity.

Teachers and a few underemployed volunteer parents car-
pooled us back to school, where I immediately flopped onto a
beanbag chair for Sustained Silent Reading, a time of day that
only years later did I realize was as much for the teachers' benefit
as the students'. I cracked open the book, and for eight pages, I was
riveted by the adult drama. A woman named Charlotte (which
no kids I knew were named!) walked alone through an alley late
at night (which kids aren't allowed to do!). And then, on page 9,
things took a turn for the worse. Charlotte, whom I had grown
so attached to on the previous eight pages, was murdered. Twenty
years later, I still remember some vague details of the killing.
Some stabbing maybe? A thing with her spine? Maybe somebody
stabbed her with a spine? That can't be right.

At the time, however, I felt sure that each word of the description would remain vivid in my waking hours and make itself visually manifest in my dreams each night. How could anyone have
committed these words to a page? I could hardly imagine imag-
ining such violence. Physically overwhelmed by the power of the
prose, my mouth went dry and my forehead became clammy, as

if all my saliva had been wicked through my skull and converted into sweat. In a daze, I asked my teacher if I could get a drink of water.

I left the classroom, growing dizzier with every step I took, like a heroine in a Jane Austen novel realizing her betrothed had spurned her and taken another lover. Instead of turning right, toward the bubbler,[3] I walked straight across the hall, directly into the door of another classroom. Not through the door. Into it. At least I think that's what happened. I don't remember the contact, but judging from the mark it left on my face, I'm pretty sure my head slammed into the rectangular sliver of window designed not to be wide enough for hallway traffic to distract the students on the other side.

My collision with the door didn't disturb the kids in this particular classroom, though. The school I attended didn't have enough enrollees to fill its building, so it subleased part of the space to a school for hearing-impaired students. As I crashed into the door and crumpled to the ground, the deaf children remained unperturbed, but the teachers rushed into the hallway to investigate the commotion.

When my brain rejoined my body, I found myself sprawled on the floor, the two teachers from the hearing-impaired classroom hovering over me, their students peering from behind them. In the few seconds before my own teacher came to see what had happened, I remember having the thought *I am deeply humiliated by what my body just did, but also in the future I will appreciate the*

---

3   Massachusetts slang for "water fountain," pronounced *bub-blah*.

irony of this moment. It was the first time in my life I realized some-thing would make a good story. But, for years, I was too embar-rassed to tell it. Who gets light-headed from *reading*? What a dork.

I'm sure that if I read that book now, I'd laugh at the over-the-top violence, but also . . . I'm not sure of that at all. Because I've never fully managed to anesthetize myself against the macabre. Through my teenage years, my squeamishness reinforced itself in a vicious cycle. Without the exposure to more explicit imagery, I became increasingly squeamish and avoidant, which means I didn't get any more exposure, which meant I became *more* squea-mish and avoidant. My experience with horror movies, to this day, remains mostly limited to a few I saw at sleepovers when there was no tactful way to excuse myself. Every few years, I'd be caught by surprise by an unexpectedly gory piece of art (if, indeed, the film *Tales from the Hood* counts as art), and I'd revert right back to my eleven-year-old self. The fact that I didn't want anyone to see it happen to me made it all the more likely to happen.

Despite the predictable adverse reactions, I didn't stop probing the limits of my squeamishness, but I learned how to recognize and deal with these incidents. When I felt the telltale dizziness and cold sweats coming on, I'd stop what I was doing and try to distract myself from my own unspooling nerves. If that didn't work, I'd grab a glass of water and get myself as close to lying down as possible. Sometimes that meant reclining an airplane seat. Other times, under more perilous circumstances, I had to pull over my car. I never told anyone what was happening, if I could help it. And, even weirder, I almost always felt compelled to finish whatever I was reading or watching, as if narrative closure would exorcise the revulsion from my body. I had to conquer the thing that had conquered me. Weirdest of all, it often worked. I kept a library copy of Stephen King's *It* on the coffee table of my parents' den for six months, too anxious to finish it but unable to return it incomplete after a particularly eerie scene shook me up badly. Finally I picked it up, skipped four pages forward, and sped through the last three hundred. Now I can barely remember any details at all of the book that haunted me for half a year.

Finishing *It* ended my brief Stephen King phase, and yes, I realize that for a young boy whose guts were prone to pitching and curdling like a pint of heavy cream left out in the sun, having such a phase at all seems like begging for trouble. Part of me liked the spooky supernatural plots (I do still like hearing people give synopses of horror movies), but a bigger part just wanted to prove that no book could get the best of me. Every time I cracked open one of his gargantuan tomes (or any of the pulpy crime novels I read as a tween), what I was really doing was testing myself, trying to prove my strength. It was never an attempt to push my external boundaries. Books were never off-limits to me. I just wanted to know if I'd finally put the worst of my trembling, childish reactions behind me. Sometimes it seemed like I had. Other times, the dizziness returned, my loins seemingly ungirdable.

"I just need to sit down," I'd say to whoever was around me when I grew overcome. "I'll be fine in a second." And I always was, physically, fine. Emotionally, I felt a deep shame. I was still a dizzy little fifth-grade dweeb, not only unable to navigate the world but actually ill at the mere *thought* of its horrors. I was embarrassed that I needed to be cared for. For not being able to handle something no one else seemed to have a problem with. For having the fragile disposition of an orchid or a child king. No one could know what was really the matter, I decided.

The last time I fainted was, somehow, more embarrassing than the time I smashed headfirst into a classroom full of deaf fifth graders. I was on a crowded subway train, headed downtown from my apartment in Harlem toward a part of Manhattan that used to be Harlem until so many white people moved in that they stopped calling it that. I was listening to a podcast in which two comedians were discussing their preferred porn genres in graphic detail. I hadn't set out to hear this conversation; it's just where the interview went. This was something I objectively should have been able to hear, not just as a *guy*, but as a *human* who understands that life is created through sexual intercourse (although probably not any of the acts being described on the podcast in question).

Cold perspiration beaded across my forehead. Knees buckling, I slid into one of the subway car's few empty seats, much to the dismay of the older Dominican women boarding the train. In a perfect world, I would have sat for another fifteen minutes and composed myself. In a *more* perfect world I wouldn't have made myself queasy listening to a conversation about sex. Alas, this is the world we've been born into, so neither of those options presented themselves to me. At my scheduled stop, reality still gelatinous and quivering, I got off the train, climbed a flight of stairs, and collapsed onto the floor of the subway station, a surface so disgusting that even the city's rats douse their paws in Purell after touching it.

My father once told me that the key to getting treated quickly in an emergency room is to lie flat on the floor, because they know you wouldn't do that unless your situation was really dire. Similarly, if you ever need assistance in a New York City subway station, simply crumple to the ground. People will stop to check on you, which is remarkable, considering that in New York, the penalty for standing still to look at your phone in the middle of a crowded sidewalk is death.

In the movies, someone garnering the sympathy of hardened New Yorkers is heartwarming. In reality, it felt demoralizing, an admission of weakness. It felt like a mob boss deciding that murdering a snitch is beyond contempt because of how pathetically he begged for his life, or a referee calling off a boxing match after one overmatched fighter's eyes have swelled shut. The kindness of strangers in New York City is truly the pity sex of compassion. When it's presented to you, you take it, because you know you need it. But you don't want to rely on it the way that circumstances have forced you to. At least, I didn't.

Me, an adult man who faints on the subway.

That was the shame I felt as I slumped to the floor in the movie theater lobby, hopeful that as long as I didn't keel fully over, I'd avoid attracting the concern of people walking by. Just before *Gone Girl* ended, Maris stepped out into the lobby, looking confused. I waved from my seat on the horrible carpet.

"Why are you down there? Are you okay? Do you need anything?"

"Actually, a bottle of water would be amazing. I'll be okay. I'll explain in a minute." I gave a weak smile and handed her four dollars, the amount you would pay for water in a movie theater or anywhere after the apocalypse. She came back and handed me the bottle, and I took a sip. Then I told her the whole story. About the door and the deaf kids and the dizziness and most recently the gurgling. She smiled.

"I was worried you'd left or something."

"Sorry. My phone died."

"I'm just glad you're okay."

"But wait. What happened?" I asked. She looked confused again. "With Gone Girl. What happened?"

"Oh! She went back to live with Ben Affleck. They were kind of stuck together." Thankfully, she'd already read the book.

A Few of My Greatest Fears, in No Particular Order

Getting stabbed in the face; specifically, the eye.

Desperately needing to get to a bathroom on one of those days when the subway just stops indefinitely for no apparent reason.

Footage of the all-white production of *Once on This Island* that my high school put on making it online.

Getting my wedding ring caught on something and having it almost rip my hand off, like happened to Jimmy Fallon. (Don't Google it.)

Anyone who respects me finding out that I thought paisley was a color until I was like twenty-seven.

Something bad happening to my wife or parents while I am traveling for work.

Turning into one of those old guys who's like, "I don't get why things are different from when I was a kid! Everything should stay the same, starting at the point when I became comfortable with it!"

America continuing its horrifying trend of race- and gender-based income inequality, leading to even more wealth and opportunity being concentrated in the hands of an even smaller group, leaving everyone else unprepared for the consequences of climate change, automation, and other accelerating global challenges.

Being kicked by a horse.

1-800-GOOD-PORN

As my friends and I gained small measures of independence, we also gained smaller measures of disposable income, and our recreation became increasingly rooted in practical jokes. So even though I had no aptitude or stomach for pranks, as a teenager I couldn't avoid getting caught up in them.

My parents' house was the closest to our middle school of all my friends' homes, so most days a small crew of miscreants tumbled through our front door to play video games (*Mario Kart 64* and *GoldenEye 007*, to be specific and dated) and talk about boobs (and other things, too), before dispersing to their own residences to do or ignore their homework depending on what they wanted out of life.

One day, in the middle school cafeteria, a friendly acquaintance named Garren revealed that through some unspecified mechanism he had discovered that if you dialed the number 1-800-GOOD-PORN, you would reach the desk of a man named Al Weaver at a company called Weaverson and Associates (or perhaps

Weaver, Son, and Associates . . . it was hard to tell over the phone). And if you asked Al Weaver if you could purchase or simply hear more details about the GOOD PORN promised by his office's phone number, he would go absolutely ballistic.

Well, this all sounded pretty great to me and my friends, who had ample free time in the afternoon and no ability to drive or convince girls to make out with us, our two loftiest aspirations at the time. Fortunately, anything that moved the hands of the clock from three until six p.m. that didn't improve our brains, bodies, or spirits was fair game, and pissing off a white-collar worker in a random city fit the bill of an afternoon's entertainment.

That afternoon, a bunch of us gathered in my parents' kitchen, forming a tight semicircle around the phone bolted to the wall at eye level. A bolder teen than I carefully dialed *67 to block my parents' number from being recognized by Al Weaver's caller ID (assuming Weaverson and Associates was equipped with the service in the first place). He then punched in 1-800-GOOD-PORN, amid much giggling and many muffled *shut up shut up shut up*s.

The phone rang. It rang again.

"Al Weaver, Weaverson and Associates."

"Hi, I was wondering if you could [*giggling fit*] shut up shut up shut up. I was wondering if you could tell me more about your [*giggling fit*] shut UP . . . good porn. [*Giant eruption of laughter.*] Shut up!"

"Sorry, that's not something I can do."

"Are you sure you can't tell me more about your good porn?" [*Sustained giggles.*]

"I'm quite sure. Goodbye, now. Have a good day."

[*Asphyxiating fit of laughter.*]

And so it went, every weekday, for what must have been a month. We'd stop at my house after school and call Al Weaver as routinely as you might call a loved one after a flight to tell her that your plane landed safely. It was reflexive, and soon he came to expect us. When you receive a phone call once a day for four straight weeks inquiring about your good porn, those moments, I imagine, tend to stand out.

Here's the problem with pranks, though: the joke lands only if the person whose expense it is at actually feels bad. If the prankee takes his pranking in stride, there's nothing to laugh at. I don't even really like surprise parties, which are just pranks with cake at the end. You have to lie to someone you love just to trick them into attending a birthday party that you could have told them about in the first place. A birthday party isn't better if you don't know about it. It's exciting for a few seconds, and then you realize you're dressed all wrong because you thought you were going to the movies or out for barbecue.

Fortunately/unfortunately, Al Weaver was a perfect prank call victim. He bore our torment with responses that were by turns exhausted, inconvenienced, and irate. But he had no choice. Because we were calling from a blocked number, we could have been legitimate clients. But we never were. It was always a group of four to eight middle school students, with the same request. In some respects, I'm not sure why he got quite so upset. Our calls took up, at most, thirty seconds of his day. We rarely tried again if he hung up early.

On the other hand (though it took me years to realize this), he probably had *no idea* why we were calling and asking for "good porn." It had nothing to do with his name, his job, or his company. Garren had stumbled on 1-800-GOOD-PORN by dialing phone numbers he thought were funny. Al Weaver could have thought of his phone number as 1-800-GOOF-RORO or 1-800-HOOD-SOSO or simply 1-800-4663-7676.[1] He could not possibly have intuited the game we were playing.

So it continued. I was a little nervous about getting caught when my parents got the next phone bill, but I couldn't stop what we'd started. The momentum was too great. I was too scared to place the calls myself, but each afternoon, I let my friends into the house, ushered them into the kitchen, and took part in our daily ritual.

Until one day, we got sloppy.

At first, everything seemed to go according to plan. We called Al Weaver. We asked him for porn. We laughed at him. He hung up in a huff. We hung up and laughed more. But something was different on this day.

As soon as we put the receiver down, my parents' phone started to ring. We stopped laughing. We stared. I didn't have to pick up to know the truth: it was Al Weaver.

"Hello?" I said, as I put the phone to my ear. I did not have to remind my friends to stay quiet. An electric silence filled the room.

---

1   I have no idea why Al Weaver's phone number was eight digits long instead of seven. Probably the calls just started after the R of GOOD-PORN and we never noticed. Or someone did notice and kept it to himself because it would have spoiled the joke.

"Hello?" replied Al Weaver's reedy voice from his office in (we assumed, for some reason) Kansas. "Is this the man of the house?"

I cleared my throat and made my voice as deep as it could go, which was not very deep. "Uhh, yes. Yes it is."

"Well, sir. Please tell your son and his friends to stop bothering me at work. Can you do that for me?" he snapped.

"Yes. Certainly I can tell my son that," I replied, in my best imitation of how one adult talks to another adult, man to man, when they want to resolve a problem. (I was probably imitating how Tim "the Tool Man" Taylor talked to his neighbor Wilson through the fence on *Home Improvement*.)

"Well, good," he asserted.

"Yes, good," I confirmed, like a grown-up.

I hung up the phone. Someone must have forgotten to dial *67, and because of that we could never call 1-800-GOOD-PORN again. In part the calls ended because Al Weaver had my phone number. Even if we wanted to prank him from a blocked number somewhere else, he'd still think it was coming from my house. He could call back at any time and talk to my actual dad instead of me doing my best generic dad impression. But perhaps the bigger issue was, the power balance had shifted. Al Weaver had gone on the offensive. He was no longer afraid of us and our bizarre demands for adult entertainment. The spell of the prank was broken.

A Technicality

About half a mile from school was a convenience store whose regular clerk's give-a-shit meter was calibrated such that he wouldn't sell us *Playboys*, but he'd overlook the store's eighteen-plus policy on cigarette lighters.

Once we realized this, we all bought lighters of our own. A couple of guys started smoking. I'm pretty sure that if you can grow a goatee in eighth grade you are legally obligated to start smoking. The rest of us just enjoyed setting things on fire. We set flame to anything flammable: Plastic bottles that dissolved in the heat like they'd looked directly at the Ark of the Covenant. Pools of lighter fluid. Plastic bottles filled partway with lighter fluid. I'm pretty sure there's a hole in the ozone layer directly above the parking lot behind our local shopping center.

Once, my parents found a small Bic lighter in a pair of my jeans. My dad asked me what it was for.

"It's not for smoking," I explained. "Sometimes we set things on fire."

"Well, don't do that," he said.

So I stopped setting things on fire. I just stood nearby while the other kids did.

You Don't Know, Now You Know

The summer after eighth grade, my friends and I returned for our last year at Camp Shalom. It was the end of an era, if not for the camp, at least for our little clique. The core of our group of friends was composed of me, Ethan, Barry, Eric, Aaron, Matt, and Dan. By our final year, we had very little interest in summer camp, but it was the only place we could go to hang out all day under some kind of nominal supervision. Other than our general lack of *spirit*, we caused very little trouble. Between the seven of us, we have spent very little time in prison, and we averaged a pretty decent score on our SATs. As you might expect from the name of the camp, we were all Jewish, except Matt, who was Jewish-ish (slightly anxious and a picky eater).

Many of us had started at Shalom after our first year of elementary school. That initial summer, as a seven-year-old, I fractured my wrist playing the camp's signature game of volleybat, which was just baseball with a volleyball. Playing shortstop, I tried to stop a screaming line drive hit by my counselor, and the force of the ball broke my bone. Clearly, supervision was lax. I'm left-handed. It's ridiculous that I was playing shortstop in the first place. It was a testament to the friendships we formed that I came back to camp the following summer, never mind six more.

Most of us attended our final year as counselors-in-training, or CITs. Too young for real summer jobs, but too pubescent for another year as campers, we spent our days assisting counselors, and our parents paid for the experience.

Our tasks as CITs were varied: escorting campers to and from the bathroom, hauling sporting goods from equipment sheds to various fields and courts, cleaning up the messes that the camp's single custodian didn't have the time to attend to. For two weeks when the drama instructor just didn't show up, I happily took her place. I guided the youngest campers through improv and imagination games. I allowed the eleven- and twelve-year-old boys, who refused to sit still, to have structured insult competitions, funneling their instinct for bullying and disrespect into a creative writing project.

My worst day on the job came when the camp director handed me and two other friends a bottle of Pine-Sol and a pair of shovels, and directed us to move several pizzas into a Dumpster from the ground directly next to the Dumpster where someone else had left them after a camp-wide party *three weeks before*. Any effect the cleanser had was purely psychosomatic. We'd have had better results huffing the cleaning fluid than we did splashing it on the garbage. That morning, the concept of "dry heaving" went from something I'd read about to something I could describe firsthand.

Because we weren't getting paid, we took every opportunity to

disappear to far-flung corners of the camp and ditch our respon-
sibilities. Basically, we did whatever we wanted until a higher-up
yelled at us to do our jobs. We never faced any real threat of ter-
mination because we provided the camp with both labor and rev-
enue.

Most often, we'd sneak down to the basketball court for
games of three-on-three, knockout, and ultimate footsketball (a
football/basketball/Ultimate Frisbee hybrid we'd invented). But
we had other, more subtle tactics for shirking our jobs, too. We
would pretend to sweep the floor of the nurse's cabin, where our
friend Laura was pretending to be sick. We'd hang out in the
woods, spending hours discussing camp minutiae and pop culture
hypotheticals, like "Did you hear that two counselors had sex in
a rowboat in the middle of the lake last week?" or "Do you think
that stoner kid from the oldest boys bunk who didn't come back
this summer could have died from an overdose of pot?" and "Can
you even overdose on pot?" to *deeply* hypothetical questions such
as "Which members of our friend group would be which members
of the Wu-Tang Clan?" I aspired to be GZA. Not the biggest star,
but, as Method Man once said, "We form like Voltron, and GZA
happen to be the head." That could be me, I thought. The nerd
brain of a fighting cartoon robot.

We'd discovered Wu-Tang the year before, in our final summer
as campers. And sure, *discovered* is kind of a strong word, considering the group had already put out two classic albums plus half a
dozen or so solo records from its individual members. It took four
years for the group's debut album, *Enter the Wu-Tang (36 Chambers)* (nine members of the group, nine hearts, four chambers per

heart, if you were wondering about the numerology) to find its way into our hands. Once it did, we practically wore a hole through the CD.

Our favorite track was "Wu-Tang Clan Ain't Nuthing ta F' Wit." The chorus consisted of what sounded like every member of the group chanting in unison, "Wu-Tang Clan ain't nuthing ta *fuck* with!" until they figured the listeners had gotten the point.

At nine members strong, the group formed an eclectic and unwieldy hip-hop collective. Each Clan affiliate distinguished himself with a signature vocal tone and style. Ghostface Killah's rhymes raced toward you like a fire truck, sirens blaring, barreling down an empty street. Method Man's gritty swagger could sand a tree stump into a dinner table. Ol' Dirty Bastard crooned and rambled as if he'd never heard music before but had heard *of* it. Their songs could consist of half a dozen verses and barely the hint of a chorus, committed to record with the frenzied intensity of an organized crime syndicate destroying evidence. The name Wu-Tang comes from the group's collective obsession with kung fu movies, although to the best of my knowledge, none of the members personally claim Asian heritage.

Whenever we listened to Wu-Tang, one member of our social circle, often me, sat beside the portable stereo, quickly twiddling the volume knob to censor the myriad F-words and N-words. And, depending on how closely we were being supervised, the S-words and A-words as well. Earlier that year, Ol' Dirty Bastard had rushed the stage at the Grammys to proclaim "Wu-Tang is for the children!" but the director of my Jewish Community Center summer camp would likely have disagreed.

At the very least, Wu-Tang was for *different* children, ones without the luxury of youthful naivete. Kids who had already learned that life is unfair, and it's unfairer for some people more than others, and that bad things happen not at random but for reasons beyond their control (or their parents', for that matter). Kids who dealt with adult problems much earlier in life, and who needed the vocabulary to express that terrible knowledge.[1]

Our counselor that summer was a kid named Eli. Eli was the camp's surliest counselor, and the biggest. He stood over six feet tall, an anomaly among teenage Jews. He couldn't have been more than six years older than the rest of us, but he felt less like a babysitter than a deadbeat dad. Eli was just as likely to wander away from our assigned activities as we were, and he happily turned a blind eye (or, more accurately, a deaf ear) to whatever music we had blasting from our boom box.

I grew up in a homogenous suburb of Boston; MC Hammer was pretty much the first Black person I was even aware of. Ethan, my best friend in kindergarten, had the "U Can't Touch This" cassingle. He brought it in for show-and-tell one day, and to five-year-old me, it was like hearing Jimi Hendrix play the national anthem.

I loved the song immediately. Of course I did. MC Hammer was exactly what a five-year-old would think was cool, even if he

---

1   Obviously, the music wasn't all heartbreak and violence. It was also a lot of fun. The joy and the danger existed side by side, a dichotomy the rapper Notorious B.I.G. summed up in a single song title: "Party and Bullshit." He was a much more succinct writer than I am.

hadn't also been the star of a cartoon show in which he wore magic shoes.[2] In real life, he rapped in the very friendly way you had to, to make it past Tipper Gore. He wore shiny, billowing pants, like he lived on a pirate ship from outer space. Even his lyrics were both appropriate for and intelligible to children. As a kindergartner, "You can't touch this!" was something I was told a lot, about everything from the stove to, fittingly, the stereo itself.

MC Hammer's songs (okay, fine . . . song, singular) didn't sound like what my parents listened to; the music was faster, brighter, *younger*. He was not (as no one can be) the voice of *the* Black experience in America, but he definitely represented a different point of view than I'd heard before. Hammer didn't sing like on the Dire Straits or Bonnie Raitt tapes my mom and dad played on car trips. There were no endless, ouroboros guitar solos like on my dad's Grateful Dead bootlegs. The music was simple and propulsive (the sample, of course, came from Rick James's "Super Freak," but I wasn't aware of that at the time; I just thought MC Hammer was a goddamn funk genius), and the words were staccato and conversational.

It wasn't *good* rapping, per se. The first couplet of "U Can't Touch This" pairs "hard" and "lord," two words that do not, in fact, rhyme. But my tiny brain, steeped since birth in classic rock, wasn't ready for *good* rap music yet. Dr. Dre's *The Chronic* came out less than three years after *Please Hammer, Don't Hurt 'Em* (a request that may have actually been more necessary than it sounded, given the gang members that accompanied Hammer as

---

2   Which he was/did.

muscle), and if I'd heard the Dre album in its entirety, it probably would have given me nightmares for the entirety of elementary school. Besides, where would I have even heard of Dr. Dre at the time? Everyone I knew was also a white person from suburban Boston, and they were all either six or forty years old, not exactly the "Fuck tha Police" demographic.

There are people who don't like or listen to rap now, but in the 1990s as the East Coast/West Coast feud was in full swing, white people in the suburbs were racistly *terrified* of it, specifically any music that bore the ominous label of "gangsta rap." The news coverage of Snoop Dogg's murder trial made it seem like he was going to come out of the TV and pull a gun on the viewer. So, for the time being, I stuck to the gentler stylings of Hammer, Vanilla Ice, and the New Kids on the Block (to a five-year-old Jewish kid in 1990, NKOTB was rap). Those artists were safe to listen to on two levels: I wouldn't get in trouble for playing their songs, and the worlds they inhabited felt less infused with danger.

In elementary school, I continued to absorb the hip-hop that made it all the way to the center of the mainstream. My parents submitted to *some* rap. They didn't raise any objections to hearing "Gangsta's Paradise" by Coolio on Mix 98.5 alongside more mom-friendly hits like Joan Osborne's "One of Us." Or at least not any more than they rolled their eyes at "Tubthumping" by Chumbawamba. But by middle school, I'd begun branching out. I soon came to realize that there were actually two genres of hip-hop: the stuff my parents knew I listened to, and the stuff I kept from them.

The Beastie Boys bridged the gap between those two subcategories, providing catchy, inescapable radio singles as well as weirder and more explicit album tracks. Mike D., MCA, and Ad-Rock ushered me into the hip-hop of a post–MC Hammer world. Sure, it was rap, but it was goofy and Jewy. It sounded like music made by me and my friends, plus time, plus turntables, plus talent, plus beer. By the time we really got into the Beasties' catalog in the late 1990s, they'd already transitioned from (fighting for their right to) party animals to reflective but still silly rap elder statesmen. They wore fake mustaches and fought cheesy Godzillas in their videos. And I think it helped that, like Hammer (and it hurts to admit this), they weren't *that* good at rapping. "If you try to knock me, you'll get mocked / I'll stir fry you in my wok" is, with hindsight, not the Pulitzer-worthy couplet I thought it was in eighth grade.

I was thirteen when the Beastie Boys released *Hello Nasty*, their first album since I started buying albums on my own. Beginning there and backtracking through the Beasties' catalog, I became ravenous for hip-hop music. At least once a month a small group of my friends from school and I walked to our local record store (even at the time an antiquated term) to seek out new music. We timed our purchases carefully. Some of the employees narrowed their eyes at tweens attempting to buy CDs bearing the stark black-and-white PARENTAL ADVISORY: EXPLICIT LYRICS sticker.[3] But not Abe.

Abe encouraged our forays into explicit content, whether it was heavy metal or an R-rated movie.

---

3   The cover of one George Carlin album features a giant parental advisory label covering 80 percent of its surface, with the comic's head barely poking over the top.

"Are you psyched for Rammstein?" he leaned forward over the counter to ask, as a friend slid the new disc by a German heavy metal band across the counter at him. He always said "psyched." Abe was the least famous person I've ever heard of who had his own catchphrase.

"Are you psyched for this VHS copy of Kevin Smith's *Mallrats?*"

"Are you psyched for this 'Mean People Suck' keychain?"

Abe was our hype man, but more than that, he served as our guide to the world of grown-up entertainment—although, like my camp counselor Eli, he couldn't have been that much older than we were. His approval made us feel like we were making cool, adult choices. Abe continued to encourage us even after our tastes began to diverge. My middle school friends had started exploring the kind of rock music that alienated their parents. Primus. Metallica. Presobriety Red Hot Chili Peppers. But for me, it was hip-hop.

I'd return home from the strip mall and scuttle my purchase up to my bedroom. There, I'd throw the CD in the boom box on my night table and listen to it quietly. I could have plugged in a pair of headphones and cranked the volume as loud as I wanted, but something about that seemed wrong. Listening to a boom box through headphones feels a little bit like putting on a bike helmet to drive a car, a cumbersome and unnecessary amount of precaution.

Although the thumping, percussive beats grabbed my attention, I was consumed with the lyrics. I mentally cataloged the tongue-twisting consonance, incisive metaphors, and cutting slang that hadn't reached the suburbs yet. I had a particular affinity for

East Coast artists who blended hard truths with wry humor and occasional whimsy. Biggie, Nas, A Tribe Called Quest, Redman. The words shot into my brain and unspooled like a busted cassette. I unpacked and understood them little by little. When I first heard the lyric "I never sleep / 'Cause sleep is the cousin of death," it hit me like the first time you see your own blood. Of all the anxieties that had kept me up at night over the years, it had never occurred to me that *sleep itself* was the enemy. *How close a cousin is it?* I wondered. *And what do you do all night if you never sleep?*

I also kept careful track of the curse words, specifically where they differed from the radio and music video versions. It was exhilarating to hear the artists express themselves outside the strict rules of radio edits. Juvenile's omnipresent "Back That Thang Up" of course became "Back That Azz Up" when freed from the confines of the FCC. The radio edit of Eminem's breakout hit, "My Name Is," (an embarrassingly important song to me at the time) altered whole swaths of its explicit taunts and mocking threats to make it presentable for mass consumption. I came late to the Notorious B.I.G.'s landmark debut, *Ready to Die*, and for years I'd heard only the radio-friendly version of "Juicy," whose chorus contained the pithy but inoffensive incantation: "If you don't know, now you know." On the album version, Biggie punctuates that statement with an emphatic N-word. The lyric took me by surprise: I didn't know, and then I knew.

Clearly, that song wasn't made for *me*. Biggie's word choice drove the point home. It wasn't just the diction that revealed I wasn't the target audience for a lot of my favorite music. Off the same Notorious B.I.G. album, one of the most haunting tracks,

"Things Done Changed," contrasts the vibrant, almost quaint past of Biggie's Bed-Stuy neighborhood in Brooklyn against its harrowing present. In light of the increasing levels of violence, he even feels nostalgic for the days of settling disputes with fists instead of guns. "Instead of a MAC-10, he tried scrappin' / Slugs through his back and / That's what the fuck happens." Once I figured out what that meant, I knew it reflected the coldness of circumstances I'd never experienced firsthand. Still, I was riveted by the writing, the charisma, the attention to detail, and of course the wicked loud drums.

While my middle school friends mostly stuck to rock and roll,[4] my Jewish summer camp friends were into rap as well. I don't know whether it was the vicarious access the Beastie Boys gave us to cities like New York and Los Angeles from our bedrooms in the suburbs, or our experience as outsiders in towns populated largely by Boston-area Protestants and Catholics, but something about the music made sense to our teenage brains.

Our summer camp clique faced the traditional Jewish encouragement to excel at academics, to pore over texts and uncover new meanings; while we were getting into rap music, we were also studying for our bar mitzvahs. Both pursuits involved learning and parsing dense, opaque lyrics. Only one of them actually felt like it related to the rest of our lives and would help us breach the boundary between boyhood and manhood.

Rap was and is at its roots a refusal to stay within the margins

---

4   Some kids in my grade listened to hip-hop, for sure, but we ran in different social circles.

prescribed for you and a celebration of culture that's not taken seriously by the mainstream. It's aggressive and silly and sincere and profane. And, just like most teenagers, even summer camp Jews, a lot of it projected an air of invincibility and irreverence even in the face of venerated institutions. Even if we didn't always feel that way ourselves, we could aspire to it.

The music tapped into every teenager's desire to live like a human middle finger. We were "nice Jewish boys," but even nice kids realize that a lot of the world is often unkind and unfair. And sure, we lacked the swag (as the kids say, unless they don't anymore) of 2Pac flipping off the camera, but it felt inspirational that *someone* was out there, calling bullshit in ways we only wished we could.

Of course, 2Pac was about more than just flipping the bird to photographers and bragging about having sex with other rappers' wives. His music also touched on the ravages of poverty, the horrors of violence, and the importance of loving your mom. Of those topics, only the third one felt particularly germane to my life at the time. Though we felt a sincere sense of powerlessness, it was not because we were disempowered; it was because we were children. There was no sinister machine for us to rage against.[5] And despite any cultural divide we may have felt between ourselves and swaths of our classmates, we were visually (and for the most part, economically) indistinguishable from them.

There were differences, though, for me specifically. While the rest of my camp friends attended schools with clusters of other

---

5 We were also listening to a lot of Rage Against the Machine around this time.

Jewish students, I was one of maybe ten at mine. As a younger kid, it felt kind of fun and special to be different. My mom came into my first-grade class to read the story of Hanukkah. I was proud to share my family history and tradition with the other seven-year-olds. But that feeling evaporated in middle school, where the two least cool things you can do are "be different" and "hang out with your parents." Judaism still figured prominently in my identity, but it had also become a hassle. I didn't want to explain Passover anymore. I was sick of running from classroom to classroom after the Jewish high holidays, asking teachers for the assignments that I, one of maybe three students who had been out of school on those days, had missed. I even worked in a local church nursery taking care of the kids too young to sit in services, which felt like the ultimate example of acceptance without belonging.

Now, obviously, working in entertainment and living in New York City, I come across guys like me all the time. Brooklyn is awash with secular Jews in their early thirties wearing A Tribe Called Quest T-shirts and retro Jordans. The bars teem with would-be Beastie Boys. On many nights I feel the exact inverse of my middle school self-consciousness. *Ugh. Why is everyone here just like me?*

Most nights in my early teenage years, I fell asleep to the underground rap block on the radio station broadcast from Emerson College, ten miles away in downtown Boston. I listened from a cocoon of my own whiteness, insulated in my parents' house, nestled in a quiet middle-class suburb, a turducken of safety and privilege.

At the time, I took that all for granted: growing up with economic security, in a society where racial bias worked in my favor. Even when I started going to concerts with my friends, being a young man meant I never felt unsafe traveling into and out of the city late at night. These are all things I try to be mindful of now, but I just hadn't been exposed to much else at the time. Or, when I had, I'd lacked the awareness to recognize that what separated me from anyone else wasn't an inherent goodness, but the good luck of being born where, who, and when I was.

Rap accelerated my awareness of the wider world. It showed me how much I didn't know. The ultimate example of the chasm between my life and the world transmitted to my eardrums by the laser in my Discman was that by the time I listened to Biggie's first album the whole way through, he'd already been shot to death, a victim of the kind of violence he so vividly described on the record. 2Pac had been murdered the year earlier.

While the music we listened to created an aura of bravado, strength, and recklessness in the face of death, the crushing weight of circumstances was impossible for the artists to avoid. Meanwhile, hundreds of miles away, *we* were the invincible ones, lacking in swagger but immune to and unafraid of the most brutal realities of America.

But our last summer at camp, we learned that we were also mortal.

In the middle of August of that year, a white supremacist fired seventy bullets at a Jewish Community Center in California, injuring five people. This was the late 1990s, before the pure desperate grief of a mass shooting was tempered with the frustrated resignation of "this is just what happens sometimes." The next

day, camp wasn't canceled, but the directors shepherded all the
kids to the field farthest from the front gate. Then, as an additional security precaution, the higher-ups stationed Eli at the
camp's entrance.

Eli was not exactly a model employee on days when the stakes
weren't life and death. He had only one qualification as a security
guard: his sheer size. His flaws were that he wasn't bulletproof
and he didn't give much of a shit about anything. Entrusting Eli
with this much responsibility seemed misguided at best. All a potential invader would have to do is wait until Eli left to get high
in the woods, and he'd be in. (Statistically speaking, it would be
a he.)

My friends and I, fourteen years old and convinced we would
never die, sneaked away from the assembly in the field and down
to the basketball courts. Eli, positioned sixty yards across the parking lot, should have sent us away, but he figured watching us play
pickup hoops beat staring at the road, wondering if every car contained a gun-toting anti-Semite. He turned his chair around to
face the court and started teasing us.

"Oh, come on!" he'd yell after a ball flew out of bounds, and
"Brick!" after a missed shot.

For obvious reasons, the camp management was on high alert
for yelling in the parking lot. Richard, the assistant director, came
running down the hill, and when he saw that no one's life was in
danger, he got pretty upset. Richard was middle aged, and we suspected he cheated at sports against the campers. He always wore
a hat to cover his bald spot, which as a kid I made fun of, but now
as a bald adult myself, just seems practical. As Richard crossed the

parking lot, Eli stood to face him, and we scurried into the woods to watch the confrontation. The exchange that followed changed the entire way I viewed authority.

"Eli! You are supposed to be *protecting this camp*, and you are not even *looking the right way*," Richard seethed.

"Hey, Rich," Eli said, "fuck you." He stood, unmoved and unimpressed. Those of us hiding in the woods, however, were thrilled. We were finally getting to see the youthful recklessness of a rap song up close.

"I . . . I . . . I am your boss and you will show me some respect," Richard sputtered. With one long arm, Eli reached out and flipped Richard's hat off his head and into a puddle.

It ruled.

"How's that for fucking respect?"

My friends and I looked at each other, mouths open in silent screams: *Did you hear that???!!?!!*

"You swear one more time, and it's your job," Richard replied. Eli stared for a long moment. We crouched in the shrubs, waiting for his response.

"Fuck, Richard." Eli paused. "Shit." Another pause. "Aaaasssssssss."

Richard picked his hat out of the puddle and shook off a few drops of hot, gross water.

"This is serious, Eli," he said, with less authority, as he turned and walked across the parking lot toward the camp's main field. Eli shrugged. He watched Richard go and then pivoted his folding chair a few degrees so he could continue heckling our basketball game.

We laughed at Eli's open defiance, but it couldn't fully penetrate the heaviness of the day. Eli's disrespect had lessened the pain of the horror across the country through his brazen and profane unwillingness to be controlled, but he couldn't erase the reality of what had happened. The shootings took place thousands of miles away, much further than the Brooklyn neighborhoods that felt so remote, reachable only through a boom box. This time, though, the trauma occurred in a place that felt like home. We had been touched by a violence we couldn't control, and the safeguards in place to protect us were makeshift at best and useless at worst. When Richard was out of sight, we headed back out onto the court, but with less enthusiasm than before.

As Biggie said: We didn't know. And then we knew. Things done changed.

Things That Make Me Feel Grown-Up (in Order of Increasing Adulthood)

Walking into a bar without getting carded.

Voting.

Writing a letter of recommendation for a friend.

Wearing a suit of my own volition.

Paying bills.

Going to bed when I get tired instead of staying up for no reason.

Not eating all the french fries if I am not hungry for all the french fries.

Restraining myself from rolling my eyes at my friends' dietary restrictions.

Not knowing any of the music playing at a younger cousin's bar mitzvah or birthday party.

Cleaning something in my apartment because I noticed, on my own, that it was dirty.

Swearing in casual conversation with my parents without reprisal.

A Worthy Adversary

My first (and to date, only) nemesis was my tenth-grade Spanish teacher, Ms. Sandra Walensky. Ms. Walensky was a long-tenured teacher, beloved by many and feared by others. She wore long dresses and always seemed to be leaning slightly forward. When she was in a good mood, her posture gave her the appearance of listening intently. When she was in a bad mood, it gave you the feeling that she was about to spring forward and tackle you off your chair.

Ms. Walensky wasn't even the Spanish teacher who gave me the worst grades. Señora Griglun, my freshman- and junior-year teacher, gave really hard tests, the kind where the grades come back worse than you'd hoped, and you still feel like you got off easy. I got along great with her even when I, a grumpy, entitled nerd, felt like I should have been doing better in her class simply because I always did better in every other class.

It was not the circumstances of our meeting that made us nemeses. It was irrefutably personal. In part, it was that the way she taught was not the way I learned. Day after day, our brains rubbed each other the wrong way. We wore each other down like the thighs on a pair of corduroy pants. But more than that, she just didn't like me, and that drove me batshit berserk. How could she not recognize the delightful balance I struck? I was studious but not uptight; clever but not distracting; high achieving but not intensely competitive with my classmates. What more did she want from me?

If you are looking for a way to spin my psyche out into parking lot doughnuts of desperation, all you have to do is hint ever so gently that you'd enjoy it more if maybe we didn't spend so much time together. I will, without fail, overcorrect whatever behavior you find unsatisfactory and send my entire personality careening in the opposite direction.

Example: Between my sophomore and junior year in college, my girlfriend at the time went back home to California for the summer. Each week, I'd send her an elaborate package featuring a letter (often written in character) and a little gift. If this sounds smothering to you, you're right! It was! My girlfriend once brought up that she found the weekly deliveries a bit *much*. I spent the next week fretting. I didn't want to disregard her input, but how else could I show I was a devoted long-distance boyfriend? The next week, I slapped a Post-it note reading "Whatever" onto a brick, crammed the brick into a flat-rate Priority Mail envelope, and mailed it to her. Was that the act of an unhinged maniac? Yes. Was it her favorite thing I mailed her all summer? Also yes. (We broke up the week the fall semester started, obviously, but we are good friends now.)

Ms. Walensky didn't just *hint* that I wasn't her favorite student, she practically announced it. She rolled her eyes when I raised my hand to ask questions. She sighed disapprovingly when handing back my homework assignments. She mocked my answers when I participated in class. Nothing I did was good or right or enough. And when I tried the opposite—laying low in an attempt to skate through our ninety-minute class unnoticed—that didn't work, either. I wasn't used to being frustrated like this by a teacher. I was supposed to be *good* at school. Sputtering through Spanish class gave me the same feeling as when you lose track of your online banking password. *How can I not crack this code?* This was supposed to be a problem for other people, not me.

Look, I used to be a teacher. All teachers want their students to learn and grow. But every teacher also has those kids who, when they're out sick for a day, inspire a silent prayer of gratitude to god, or the universe, or whichever student came back from spring break with the flu bug that's going around. For Ms. Walensky, I was that kid. I'm surprised I never walked into the classroom to find her sneezing on my midterm exam before handing it to me or rubbing an uncooked chicken breast on my desk.

My psychological breakdown began almost as soon as sophomore year started. I could have handled a bad grade or two.[1] But for a teacher to dislike me based on my personality was something I just could not abide. I wasn't always the *best* student in each of my classes, but I strove to be the *most good* in all of them. It wasn't that I was a suck-up or a teacher's pet. (I definitely was.) I

---

1   Okay, I could not have handled that.

just wanted every teacher to think I was a bright, shining star destined for greatness.

Even if I wasn't setting the curve with my test results, I wanted to make the sharpest, wittiest comments during in-class discussions and seem like the kind of kid who, if he didn't have an assignment complete, must have had a really good reason for it. And also I wanted to get, like, the second-best grades.

Most of the time, my strategy worked. I finished high school fourth in my class, which please believe me I have not brought up in at least ten years. My junior-year English teacher[2] wrote me a college recommendation so effusive about my potential that I'm slightly ashamed of becoming a medium-successful comedian and writer rather than the first Jewish pope or a newly discovered dwarf planet. (Not the astronomer who discovered the dwarf planet, the thing itself.)

Ms. Walensky, however, was neither charmed by my personality nor impressed by my classwork. She had no interest in my clever asides or digressions, and no level of conversational fluidity or grammatical expertise with the Spanish language could convince her that I was a dedicated student. It was worse than getting bad grades. Bad grades reflect poor work. This was about my personality, which I believed at the time to be excellent. Although, almost as upsettingly, my grades in Ms. Walensky's class were also not stellar.

From the beginning of the year onward, she gave homework

---

2   Ms. Norelli, who taught Faulkner so brilliantly that she tricked me into thinking I liked Faulkner. I didn't! I just liked her!

assignments that I found inane, and I struggled to complete them. Tasks like, "I want two pages of work, front and back, on textbook pages fifty-five through fifty-seven." Sometimes the book had practice exercises on the pages she assigned, but she directed us not to focus too much on those. Other times, she would point us to a table of contents, the title page for a new chapter, and a list of ten vocabulary words.

"What do you want us to do?" we asked, at first.

"Whatever you want. Just make sure it's two pages, front and back."

At first, I did my best to complete her busywork. I wrote practice sentences with unfamiliar vocabulary words. I did the exercises the textbook editors prescribed. I was used to putting in the effort with assignments that I found challenging (except trigonometry. Fuck triangles, and fuck their whole crew. Fuck cosines, fuck sines, and especially fuck tangents.) and coasting through tasks that were easy. I wasn't accustomed to education as an exercise in volume of work done. But it was my homework, so I did it. Because I wanted to be the most good.

Then, gradually, Ms. Walensky stopped checking our assignments, and I lost my goddamn mind. I'd spend two hours staring at the pages of my textbook and free-associating to fill the blank pages. *I would have liked to show you the turtle. She would have liked to give me the tomato. We would have liked to throw them the chinchillas.* It quickly grew repetitive and incoherent, like the verses of a Red Hot Chili Peppers song. And then to show up in class and have the teacher not even validate the effort? Screw that. I wanted to stand up on my chair and display my work to her like Rafiki presenting Simba on Pride Rock. *Do you see this? Do you*

see what a good kid I am? Gaze upon my works and . . . I don't
know . . . put a little check mark on the top of the page.

I complained about my situation to anyone who would listen.
My parents. My classmates. Friends at other schools with no frame
of reference.

"She just doesn't like boys," said my friend Cate with a shrug
at play rehearsal, in response to my lamentations. Cate was a year
ahead of me and was in her second consecutive year of Spanish
with Walensky. She was one of the teacher's favorites, a hardwork-
ing student with a studious disposition. Her words brought me
some comfort. Maybe it wasn't *me*. Maybe I was being prejudiced
against because of my gender. What a relief. And, as a high school
boy, I probably deserved some level of skepticism and distrust.
"Just do the work and you'll be fine," Cate assured me.

Still, over time I let my work slip. Once, the only paper I'd had
on hand was college ruled, so it had twice as many lines as the
wide-ruled notebook sheets we usually worked with. So, to compensate, I did a page and a half of homework instead of two. It
worked out to the same amount of lines, but because it wasn't two
full pages, I didn't earn full credit. I became despondent, and my
effort continued to erode. Some nights I started doing one page
front and back, and then read ahead in the textbook. Or I wouldn't
read ahead. Or I'd just do one side of a page because nothing mat-
ters so why bother?

My final breaking point came in our last Spanish class before
winter break. Ms. Walensky had prepared a lesson on holiday tra-
ditions around the world. "Does anyone know how mistletoe was
originally used around Christmas?" she asked the class.

I raised my hand. "Well, back in the day, if you didn't like someone, you'd take a little mistletoe and sprinkle it in their egg-nog, then . . . boom," I joked, caught up in the holiday spirit.

Ms. Walensky stared at me, revolted, the way you might look at a dog cleaning its butt with its tongue. *I know you can't help it, but you disgust me,* her face said.

"Why would you say that?" she replied. "No. Mistletoe was burned as part of a pagan ritual. It's poisonous. I bet you didn't know that," she said. Of course I *had* known that. It was the entire premise of my joke. You'd use the poison berries to murder some-one with their festive holiday beverage. (It wasn't a *great* joke, but I still stand by the fact that it makes logical sense.)

When we came back from break, things continued to deterio-rate. My every attempt to participate in class was met with wither-ing stares. She responded to any question I asked as if I'd raised my hand and commented, "Excuse me, I need to go to the bathroom, but I forget how and where to do that." The attention I paid to my Spanish homework continued to diminish. I had other things to do, and I was learning the material. Why waste my time on some-thing I'd never get credit for anyway? But my teacher's personal distaste for me caused me so much anxiety that I couldn't even enjoy the spite of disregarding her assignments.

During one homework check, Walensky was walking up and down the rows, inspecting everyone's work. Not whether it was good, whether it was simply *enough*. I dug through my backpack, desperate to come up with *any* notes I could show her. She stopped in front of my desk. I handed her my meager scribbling.

"Where is the rest of it?" she asked, knowing the answer.

"That's all I've got," I said quietly.

"Well, that wasn't the assignment."

"I think I'm having trouble figuring out how to complete the assignments to your specifications," I replied, completely worn down and desperate to figure out how to fix things. "Is there any way I could come in after class and talk about how I could do better?"

She laughed, which felt unfair, because I had said some very funny things in her class, and that was not one of them.

"The year is more than halfway over, and *now* you want help on your homework?"

"Yes."

"Well, no," she replied. And that was that.

I saw Cate at play rehearsal that night. We were chatting backstage, waiting to rehearse a scene, when for once she brought up the topic of Ms. Walensky's Spanish class. Cate seemed to have a new insight, but she was reluctant to share it.

"So . . ." she began, "I think Walensky was making fun of you in my class. She brought up someone wanting homework help this late in the year and started laughing." At that point in my life, I had very little professional experience in any field, but a teacher shit-talking a student to her other classes struck me as profoundly unprofessional.

Over the course of the year, my parents noticed my slow descent into madness (or, *en español, locura*). In part, they saw my increasing frustration as I tried to conjure up each night's two pages (which was really *four* pages, and yes, I will still die on this hill) of verb conjugations and sentence constructions engineered to showcase vocabulary words. The other, larger part of my parents' awareness of my stress was aided by my complaining.

During this period, I complained a lot. I mean, also, I complain a lot now. Not in the sense of "I'd like to speak to your manager to lodge a formal complaint." The complaining I like is the good, old-fashioned love-of-the-game kvetch, as my ancestors might have called it. It's very satisfying and even soothing when done right, like scratching a mosquito bite. There's an art to it, a delicate balance. You have to go hard enough that the itch gets taken care of, but not so hard that you make the initial problem worse. By the time winter break ended, I'd long passed the point of no return. My spirited trash talk had tipped, irreversibly, into the realm of sincere despair. I shuffled through the house, practically gnashing my teeth and rending my clothes in dread.

My mother, very generously, offered to talk to the principal on my behalf, which felt like a big deal. I didn't have what are now known as "helicopter parents," the kind who hover at all times, ready to swoop in and lift their children out of a troubling situation like the presence of danger or gluten. My folks were more like the Toyota Camry of parents. They were always steady, dependable, and there for me. But they weren't the high-speed getaway types. Aside from my dad once getting ejected from my youth basketball game for arguing with a referee who'd told me to shut up (I was probably complaining at the time), they generally advised me on how to deal with difficult authority figures rather than fighting such battles for me. So for my mom to volunteer to handle this one meant that my complaining had gone above and beyond its normal volume and frequency. For months, I demurred. I felt certain that if only I could prove to Ms. Walensky what a *good kid* I was, our tension would evaporate.

After I heard that my Spanish teacher had been making fun of me to her other classes (*en inglés*, no less!), I took my mother up on her offer. The vice-principal agreed to meet with us, and he listened to my concerns; my teacher had a personal vendetta against me, a Very Good Student, a charge that was (as far as I could tell) both concerning and clear cut. The vice-principal, a man in his fifties with graying hair, the very pinnacle of what I'd grown up picturing as a Serious Authority Figure, nodded while my mother and I took turns speaking.

When we finished detailing the abuses I'd suffered, allegations I was certain were sufficient to land my Spanish teacher in The Hague or at the very least one of those asylums for the criminally eccentric that Batman sends his enemies to, the vice-principal offered his response. Ms. Walensky, he told us, was very old. That, of course, was not news to me. But, he continued, on account of her oldness and nearness to retirement and general crankiness, this particular fight was not one he cared to pick with his employee.

My options were, as he saw them, to drop out of honors-level Spanish into an intermediate class with another teacher or suck it up and finish out the year. In short: Life's not fair. Forget it, Jake, it's Chinatown (or, in this case, Little Havana). I didn't like his decision, but I understood it. As someone who disagreed with Ms. Walensky for ninety minutes, two to three times a week, I could say for certain that confronting her was not something I'd do if I could find a way to avoid the experience.

There was no way I was going to drop the class. For one thing, that's not what a Good Kid does. For another, I was determined to propel myself through the end of the year on an engine fueled

by spite. She didn't like *me*? Well, I didn't like *her*. And unlike
my Spanish teacher, I possessed youth and vigor and a volatility
bestowed on me by my out-of-whack adolescent hormones. It's like
the adrenaline that flows through a mother's body when lifting a
car off a kid, but for slamming a door and yelling, "You'll never
understand, *Dad*!"

I should stop for a second and note here that with the benefit
of almost twenty years of hindsight, I do realize that Ms. Walensky
was not a bad person. She was, as the vice-principal said, an old
woman approaching retirement with years as a successful educator under her belt. She was also very sick, frequently missing days
and then weeks at a time of school. Even then, I didn't wish harm
on her, but every time I arrived at her classroom to find her desk
empty or occupied by an unprepared substitute, I felt an entire
snow day's level of relief concentrated into a single class period.

The endorphin rush I felt when Ms. Walensky was absent
was amplified by the fact that I had basically stopped doing my
homework assignments. I still did *some* homework. I couldn't fully
deactivate the good kid part of my brain. But I did just enough to
learn the grammar and the vocabulary that we covered in class,
and then I stopped. I figured that if I was getting scowls and repri-
sals for doing 90 percent of my homework, it couldn't get much
worse if I dropped down to a breezy 25 percent completion rate.
What would Ms. Walensky do, force-feed me mistletoe? And if she
wasn't in class to check the assignments most days, all the better.

It still felt bad that Ms. Walensky didn't like me. But even on
the days that she felt well enough to make it to school and thought
to inspect our assignments, I realized there was only so bad it could

get. Sure, her footsteps approaching my desk twisted my guts, the way a bully's fist grabs and scrunches your T-shirt so he can pull you close and let his other fist do some real damage. But once she had marked my work unsatisfactory and moved on to the next student, everything relaxed. I didn't *like* that she couldn't stand me, but I accepted it as an immutable point of fact. Once I stopped trying to convince her to get on board with the Josh Gondelman Experience (having me in her class, not a jam band I was trying to start), my life became easier and happier.

I never cut class. I have always been constitutionally incapable of not showing up places I am expected to show up. Even in college when I had mono (not from anything fun), I made it to every lecture. And I always took notes and participated in group discussions. It was important to me (outside of my willful homework negligence) to get good grades. I didn't want to screw up my GPA in a huff, and I *did* want to prove that I could learn the material without doing hours of inane busywork every night. I think, in the end, I squeaked out an A– for the year, which I took as validation of both my learning style and the endurance I displayed during our educational war of attrition.

And the sweetest part of that grade: I knew how much she hated to give it to me.

The Present-Tense Conjugation of the Spanish Verb *Nadar,* Which Means "to Swim"

(As Best as I Can Remember It)

I swim—*nado*
You swim—*nadas*
He or she swims/you (formal) swim—*nada*
We swim—*nadamos*
You (plural, in Spain) swim—*nadáis*
They/you (plural) swim—*nadan*

Screech

At my core, I am and always have been uncool, and in high school I hit my lifetime hipness nadir. I did musical theater. I was in the marching band. I didn't drink. I owned only a single pair of extremely-wide-leg[1] JNCO pants, and they were bile-colored corduroys. During my brief tenure on the junior varsity basketball team (my only traditionally cool extracurricular), instead of high-top sneakers, I wore throwback Adidas Superstars. Instead of wearing prescription goggles, I got a pair of thick black Buddy Holly glasses (the kind basketball players in black-and-white photos wore before Black and white players were allowed on the same courts).

---

1 In the early 2000s, jeans width, at least where I grew up, correlated directly to coolness. Many of my classmates' individual pant legs had the girth of a country line-dancing skirt. The chicest possible outfit would have consisted of a head-to-toe denim sleeping bag with a wallet chain attached. Though true connoisseurs would notice subtle differences between the various brands, massive swaths of denim united the fashions of my high school's (white) hip-hop heads and (also mostly white) metal fans.

On one level, I liked the retro style, but on another, I wanted everyone else to know that I knew that even while playing sports, I was still kind of a dweeb.

And then there was the haircut. My springy, curly hair refused to be tamed into a JTT-style (Jonathan Taylor Thomas, for anyone who never saw the cover a *Tiger Beat* magazine in the 1990s) mushroom cut. My tips were nigh-on unfrostable. To compensate, I tried to grow an Afro, which came off kind of like accessorizing an old, beat-up car by gluing a satellite dish to the roof. I still have my first driver's license, and in the photo I look like the bass player from an all-white, all-child Parliament-Funkadelic cover band.

My peers called me "Screech," a reference to the nerdy character on the teen sitcom *Saved by the Bell*. Played by Dustin Diamond, Screech became the dork that defined dweebdom for an entire generation. He wore bright, tacky shirts. His voice cracked constantly, as if his body were an instrument through which puberty itself spoke. No boys wanted to be him, and no girls wanted to be with him (and the other way around as well).

But I had the advantage of going to a high school where *no one* was especially cool. In fact, the modest successes I achieved in my young adult life were enabled by the fact that I grew up in a small town. At the time I was in high school, Stoneham, Massachusetts, had about 23,000 residents, one of whom was an honest-to-goodness town drunk. From a numerical perspective, my high school couldn't sustain the kind of cliques you see on TV. Nearly everyone played multiple roles, so it was hard to stereotype. Star soccer players acted in the spring musical. Stoners competed on the math team. Our student body blurred the lines of high school social strata like the goth cheerleaders from Nirvana's "Smells Like Teen Spirit" video.

Because the social circles at my high school were constantly overlapping to form social Venn diagrams, it didn't seem especially unusual that the class elected officials, from president on down, had two disparate jobs: they planned the proms and dances, and they wrote a comedy sketch for Carnival Ball.

What the hell is Carnival Ball? you are probably wondering, unless we went to high school together. (And if we did: Hi, Mark!)

Carnival Ball is, ostensibly, a talent show. It lasts three hours. Although, in the same way that a windchill factor makes the air feel colder, a parade of sixteen-year-olds performing show tunes with fifteen-year-old piano accompanists can dilate the sensation of sitting for 180 minutes into what seems like the entire duration of the Cretaceous period. Students at all grade levels audition with individual or group talents, mostly vocal, dance, or instrumental performances, many of which are legitimately charming on their own, if not all in a row.

Additionally, each grade puts on a comedy sketch. The sketches range in duration from "a few minutes" to "the very concept of time melts away and it becomes impossible to remember what life was like before or after the sophomore class sketch." And so, because an aptitude for comedy writing was an asset to the office, I was voted class vice-president my freshman year and class president after that. My school's codification of popularity through comedy was a weird coincidence that set me on a course for my entire career. It's the kind of thing that Malcolm Gladwell would be interested in if I were way, way, way more successful.

Every spring, the Stoneham High School senior class votes for the Carnival Ball Court, which consists of ten senior boys and ten senior girls (including one of each named as the event's king and queen). The members of the court perform a choreographed ball-room dance in full formal wear to open the show. They then sit on the stage for the rest of the night, watching each act from behind, while the rest of the audience watches them watch the show. From that point on, their only real responsibility is not to be so drunk that they fall out of their chairs.

The point of this institution was never clear to me, and as an adult I have *several* questions: Was the invention of the court a trap to make sure the most popular students didn't sneak off to get each other pregnant during the marching band's rendition of the *Star Wars* theme? Was it a way for adults to gaze on the faces of youth in full bloom, remembering what they've lost? What if mem-bers of the court are gay? Isn't it weird to make them perform an elaborate heterosexuality masquerade? Why is a whole town's idea of sexuality shaped by the aesthetic of a Baz Luhrmann movie re-made with a cable access budget? I will never know the answers to any of these questions. Best-case scenario, the Carnival Ball Court is a way to make the twenty most popular students feel the prickly self-consciousness that the rest of the student body experienced every day. Worst-case scenario, the tradition descends from some kind of arranged marriage or human trafficking convention. ("You have to see how a prospective bride dances before you purchase her, after all!")

In a school short on popularity contests, it felt extra strange to devolve into a full-on feudal system for one night. Even most stereotypical high school hierarchies don't elect total lineages of nobility. Prom king and queen (which we did not have at Stoneham High) have always been the province of the clearest cool kids (or, as a prank, an outcast with psychic powers). Same for homecoming king and queen. But to expand a list to ten is almost *more* exclusive. It's easier to believe you'd be on an elite list if the list is never explicitly written out. You can always imagine you fall in the top 10 percent of the most-liked classmates until someone actually aggregates the data. As a teenager, though, everything is weird. I didn't see this event as much different from the idea of going to a prom at all or learning calculus, a discipline I spent a year of my life practicing and now can barely define.

The work I did as a class vice-president had mixed results. My participation in planning the class dance can be charitably described as "minimal" and accurately described as "probably an active impediment." I have limited aptitude for choosing complementary colors of streamers, and even less skill at hanging those streamers in a way that allows a high school cafeteria to embody a vague or impossible theme such as "A Night to Remember" or "Follow Your Dreams." In my defense, regardless of decorations, the real theme of every high school dance is dry-humping your crush in the same place you ate tater tots six hours earlier.

Fortunately, I managed to redeem my weak showing as an event planner in my execution of the other half of my duty in the class's executive branch: sketch comedy writing. When Carnival Ball came around in the spring of my freshman year, I knew I had to rise to the occasion. To make up for my shortcomings in the streamer and R&B playlist departments, I needed to step up big time if I wanted to get reelected.

Meeting number one got off to an inauspicious start. One

stipulation of each class skit was that anyone who wanted to participate had to be given a role. That meant before we hammered out a script, we had to see how many people the skit would have to accommodate. Because the freshman class had relatively few after-school commitments, and the students had not yet grown (literally) too cool for school, our adviser's classroom teemed with enthusiastic participants.

The room buzzed with unfocused energy. Despite the class officers' best attempts to corral the cast, chaos reigned. We'd settled on a basic premise ("How the Grinch Stole Carnival Ball"), but it seemed like everyone had a different vision for how to execute the idea. Entire social cliques requested to appear onstage together. One classmate insisted on incorporating his signature dance move, which, according to his demonstration, consisted of getting halfway into a headstand before falling over. After two hours, the meeting adjourned, and if anything, we'd gotten further from writing a usable script than we were when we started.

I arrived home (okay, I got a ride home from my parents) disappointed but inspired. We had the nugget of the idea, and I thought with a night's effort, I could convert that into whatever it is a nugget becomes. (Do they grow into chickens? Is that the nugget-to-chicken relationship?) Alone at my parents' computer, I needed only a couple of hours to change the words from Dr. Seuss's original text to suit the purposes of the sketch. When I showed my draft to the other class officers the next day, they had surprisingly few tweaks. My script had given everyone a moment to shine while still shoehorning the most eccentric characters into the existing structure of the Grinch's story. With just a little massaging of teenage ego ("I know this isn't the big entrance you had in mind, but sometimes less is more!") we got the cast on board.

On the day of the show, our sketch killed. I wasn't the star, but word traveled that I was responsible for the bulk of the script. On the strength of our Carnival Ball sketches (and the fact that my input never ruined a prom), I was elected class president the next three years. Senior year, I opted out of the pageantry of the Carnival Ball Court and co-emceed the show with my friends Carolyn and Emily. I never became *cool*, but in the small pool of my high school class, I was lucky to be recognized for the things I was good at. Over the next few years, I scaled back the activities I thought I *should* be doing (band, math team) as well as the ones I was never suited for (basketball) to spend more time on the extracurriculars that mattered to me.

Carnival Ball wasn't the focal point of my high school career as a performer. After playing several bit parts in *The Wizard of Oz* at the end of freshman year, I slowly integrated myself into the drama club, and by senior year, I spent nearly every afternoon at rehearsal for one of the group's three annual shows. But Carnival Ball was the first thing that gave me the confidence to realize that maybe I didn't have to preemptively acknowledge that I was a little weird or didn't fit in. Maybe who I was, was good enough, and I didn't have to apologize or make jokes about it. There was, in fact, a place I could fit in. And I had skills I could be proud of.

Most of all, Carnival Ball taught me that despite my haircut, I wasn't actually Screech.

I Hope These Years Aren't
the Best of Your Lives

Not to brag, but as president of my high school class, I got to give a speech at graduation, which is ridiculous. No high school student should speak at a graduation, for the simple fact that most of them don't know anything worth saying into a microphone. What special wisdom could I have been expected to possess? The only things I knew for sure that the adults in the audience most likely didn't know were facts that they learned in high school and had since forgotten. But the Pythagorean theorem does not exactly make for stirring oration.

I don't *regret* what I said to my high school classmates and their families, but fortunately there's no available footage of the event. And if I could talk to them now, I'd do it differently. Since I do not have access to a time machine, and my high school has not invited me back to speak to any subsequent graduating classes (what gives, SHS?), I am forced to publish that speech here.

So here's what thirty-four-year-old me would say to a group of high school students, which honestly sounds like a nightmare, but I'd do it because I'm a giver:

Good evening, Stoneham High School class of 2003. It's me, your class president. You may not recognize me, because I started losing my hair basically six months after graduation, and my metabolism slowed down right after I hit thirty, and I haven't figured out how to counteract that with diet and exercise. But who am I kidding? You'll eventually learn all this from Facebook.

Also, just a quick heads-up: in the future there's a thing called Facebook, and it helps you keep in touch with like nine people, and it's maybe destroying the world by allowing the dissemination of unfettered misinformation. No time to get into that now, though.

This is a really exciting day. Some of us will be finished with formal education as of tonight. Others will go hundreds of thousands of dollars into debt pursuing advanced degrees. At the five-year reunion, and maybe forever after, the first group will have more productive, stable lives, with families and careers firmly on track. Our guidance counselors didn't tell us that, but it's true, and it'll be a real kick in the junk to the rest of us, many of whom will be somewhat or completely adrift, despite four years spent learning about US history or psychology or, worst of all, English.

We've already come so far, though, as a group and as individuals. We've lifted each other up and consoled one another when we didn't have enough collective might to stay afloat. We learned skills and absorbed knowledge and formed friendships. Some of us even met the people we're going to spend the rest of our lives with, which is wild to me because you've only met like three hundred people. But that's none of my business. It's weird, but it's none of my business. The point is, each of us has a better sense of who we are than we did four years ago.

But, as far as we've come, we still have a long way to go. There are still so many things we need to decide. Where will we live? What will our families and communities look like? What kind of work will we dedicate our lives to? There are so many people we're still going to meet. Except, of course, for those of you who have already met the person you're going to marry. You're pretty much done with that.

· That is once again beside the point. What's important is that we have so much growth and change to look forward to. For example, it will be years before we can casually joke about 9/11. In fact, that moment feels so far off in the future that you're probably all thinking it's kind of grotesque of me to bring it up at all. I'm sorry to be a bummer, but I promise I'm right about this.

My friend Sam always says, "People say that without the bad times, you wouldn't be able to appreciate the good times, but that's not true. If you just had escalating good things happen over time, you'd always be able to appreciate them, because they would still be better than what came before."

And that's technically accurate, but it's also true that if my legs were a fish tail, I'd be a merman. Just because something is true in theory doesn't mean it's worth attempting or even possible at all. But what I do hope is that from your triumphs and the inevitable setbacks, you learn the skills you need to care for yourself and for others. Don't learn cruelty because it's efficient. Don't forsake gentleness because it's uncool. If you have strength, use it to smash through bullshit, not to punch at everything that moves.

Optimism is both more necessary and more difficult when everything seems to be crumbling around you.

So, while only an eighteen-year-old goober who has never known real hardship or enduring sorrow would wish you a life of ever-increasing joy, here's what I will say:

I hope these years aren't the best of your life. Sure, for most of us, high school was better than middle school, but that's not exactly a high bar to clear. Some of the most frustrating years of your life are the ones when you have pubes but can't drive. It's the hormonal equivalent of being all dressed up with no place to go.

And for many of us, these have been good years. Maybe we saw someone else's genitals up close for the first time. Maybe you won some kind of championship and were greeted by a roaring crowd. That's really exciting! It gets a lot harder to make people clap for you after this. Trust me. I've dedicated most of my life to it, and it's yielded mixed results.

And, even more important: if and when your life gets hard and bad for stretches, I hope that you never stop improving. Terrible things will happen to you, sometimes at random, often unpredictably. Cancer and breakups and hurricanes and shitting your pants at Thanksgiving and prejudice and dropping your cell phone in a pool don't happen to teach you a lesson or as part of a greater plan.

(Although, you should be careful with your cell phone. Eventually it will contain your entire life, and forgetting it on the kitchen counter when you leave for work will screw up your whole week. But again, there's no time for that now. Also, sorry to swear earlier. But here's something great about being an adult: swearing isn't a big deal in almost any context. It's totally fine.)

But that doesn't mean that you can't evolve with every setback. Because every time you fail, or someone fails you, you could grow embittered and defeated and withdrawn. Or you could take some time to stomp around and curse heaven and earth before making the choice to become more resolute and compassionate and righteous and tender. Just because things are bad doesn't mean you have to get worse with them.

You don't have to pretend things are good; you just have to believe they can get better.

It won't always be easy. In some cases, that will take a substantial amount of time, or effort, or support, or selective serotonin reuptake inhibitors. But you can always learn how to better stand up for yourself or for other people. You can always show up at a political protest for the first time. Every day is a new opportunity to fall in love or realize that you aren't actually in love after all.

Even at your lowest, there's always a future in which you can try a new food or stop eating a food you hate that your parents always insisted was good for you. You can become gentler and more relentless. It's not that today is the first day of the rest of your life—it's that every day you are more you than you were the day before. Your brain and heart (and the rest of your body) can grow stronger and wiser and more skillful and vibrant.

Happiness won't be possible at every moment unless you have an unlimited supply of money, a boundless appetite for cocaine, and a nonexistent fear of death. But what is always available to you is the potential to do and be better and to derive satisfaction from those improvements on their own merits. What's better than the feeling of always eating birthday cake is learning how to make a birthday cake or meeting someone who will make one for you or celebrating the birthday of someone who has, historically, gone unacknowledged. And I hope you're able to see and enjoy those opportunities, even in the face of everything and everyone who might be aligned against you.

Before I go, I'd be remiss if I didn't say this out loud for the few of you who will care: Weezer never quite makes the comeback album you want them to.

It Was Funny at the Time

During my senior year of high school, our drama club put on a forty-minute version of Shakespeare's *Much Ado about Nothing* as part of the Massachusetts High School Drama Guild's competitive theater festival (a.k.a. DramaFest, a.k.a. Fest).[1] I played Dogberry, a bumbling constable, who is portrayed by Michael Keaton in the 1993 movie version of *Much Ado*. I thought it would be funny if I shaved male pattern baldness into my hair to look more like Michael Keaton. But first, like a good kid, I asked my parents' permission.

"Well, I don't think it's a *great* idea," said my mom, "but I'm not going to tell you not to do it."

---

1 It's exactly what it sounds like. DramaFest also included a student playwriting competition, which I won my senior year. It was my first indication that maybe I could be a real writer. The summer after graduation, some friends and I put on the play in a local theater and donated all the proceeds to the high school drama club. There is a video that no one is ever, ever, ever allowed to see.

So obviously I did it. It looked, to say the least, unsettling. While my hair was growing back, I started wearing a winter hat to school. One day in the cafeteria our vice-principal told me to take it off. Didn't I know that it was against the rules? I took a deep breath and removed the hat. He recoiled in shock.

"We can make an exception," he said.

My dad, who comes by his baldness honestly, told me cryptically, "It's not always going to grow back, you know."

There's a photo of the two of us from that era sitting side by side that was funny at the time, but it becomes less so with every passing year. Time has evened our hairlines out, so they match in every picture of us now. But when I was eighteen, my hair returned in a few months, which is the only thing I miss about high school.

Don't Aim, Just Throw

When health teachers and parents and very special episodes of TV shows tell you to wait to have sex until you are in love, they are giving you bad advice. And it is bad advice I made the mistake of following.

Sleeping with someone you love is great. Sleeping with someone you love the first time you have sex is a great way to disappoint someone you love. This is especially true if that person has ever loved and/or slept with anyone else before. In that case, the thing you have saved for your first true love will wind up brief and sweaty and disappointing. Your lover will wonder whether he or she has just engaged in sexual intercourse, or missed a bus after running half a block for it and then smashed crotchfirst into a fire hydrant (not to scale).

I grew up lucky enough never to get the message that sex was something bad or dirty. But I did, over and over, receive signals that it was something for grown-ups, a thing that you'd know when it was time for, something with *consequences*, like applying for a mortgage or adopting a puppy.

"You're not ready to be having sex," my father told me offhand at one point in my midteens. At the time, he was probably right, and I took his words to heart. *My dad has had sex,* I reasoned. I was proof of that. He probably possessed some insights that I lacked. Still, both he and I spent my adolescence avoiding any deeper discussion about what those insights might be.

Our original "birds and bees" talk took only a few awkward seconds. My dad was dropping me off at a friend's house in a nearby town, and when we hit the highway, he turned down the sports talk radio that had been soundtracking our drive.

"Do you ever think about . . . you know . . . girls?" he asked. A few moments passed. I couldn't tell if he was asking if I'd started having sexual feelings, or whether he'd assumed I had and was inquiring about what gender I directed those feelings toward. In the background, men yelled at low volume about the New England Patriots.

"Uh . . . yeah," I replied. My dad nodded.

He turned the radio up, and that was that. My dad was never dishonest about human biology. We just never felt comfortable discussing it with one another. It wasn't his fault. I clammed up when the subject was broached. He may also have witnessed a dozen years of my general awkwardness and decided, "You know what, this kid won't be needing any more specific information about sexual intercourse for quite some time." He would not have been wrong to think that.

My first introduction to human reproduction came from a promo for *Roseanne*, featuring this bit of dialogue: "We met at a bar. We had sex for hours, and now I'm pregnant," said one character to another. *Duly noted,* I thought. *That's how that happens.*

My crash course in sex ed did leave out a few things, though. What "sex" was, for example. And the fact that you can have it without getting pregnant. Also, it would have been nice to know that whatever constitutes sex rarely happens for *hours* (at least, that hasn't been my experience, for which I owe any previous partners a hearty "I'm sorry" and/or "you're welcome").

In my high school every sophomore class spent an hour look-ing at the *Massachusetts Pictorial Guide to Sexually Transmitted Diseases*, which was essentially a book full of pictures of penises and vaginas and mouths and butts that looked like they'd been left in a Tupperware container in the back of a refrigerator and then forgotten for months.

One health teacher at our high school told his classes that oral sex and anal sex could result in pregnancy through a Rube Goldberg–esque series of sex acts. I don't want to get too graphic, but the likelihood of the sequence of events he described taking place was about as high as the potential for getting pregnant from playing water polo or feeding a goat.

The curriculum also subjected us to an exercise wherein every-one in the class walked around shaking hands with each other, and the twist was that if instead of shaking hands, you had been having unprotected sex, you'd have probably had full-blown AIDS already, because when you have unprotected sex with someone, it's like having sex with everyone they've ever had sex with. I mean, unless of course they used protection with previous partners. Or if you both get regularly tested between partners. Or you don't subscribe to the puritanical notion that sex is something that au-tomatically makes you *soiled forever*. But those are the things most people don't learn in school, because many teachers would rather their students be terrified virgins than well-informed managed-risk takers. And never mind the fact that somehow having sex with every person in your high school health class would be an *incredible* accomplishment in the field of ravenous bisexuality that would make David Bowie blush.

Good news for my health teachers: their plan worked on me, at least! The strategy of big-picture repression left a constant echo of fear in my adolescent brain. I internalized the drawbacks of having sex without weighing them against the benefits, which is a bad way to make decisions. It's like never going to sleep because you're too afraid you won't hear your alarm, and you'll be late for work in the morning.

The problem with trusting authority figures' proclamations that you "aren't ready" for sex is that none of them ever circle back to let you know when you *are*. Not that I would have wanted one to. Receiving an explicit signal from my dad would have felt even weirder than radio silence.

"It's time," he'd tell me, I guess, in this scenario. "Now go out there and throw it in some lucky lady . . . with her consent, of course." Obviously, that's not how my dad talks, but there's no script for the "it's time to bone, my son" speech, so I have no idea what he *would* say. Would he hand me a box of condoms with a sage nod? Would he wink while making that gesture where you move one finger back and forth through a loop you make with two fingers on your other hand? (Why is there not a word for that gesture? It's so hard to describe in writing!) It is, looking back, probably for the best that my dad didn't try to give me the green light for coitus.

I'm relieved that my authority figures didn't bombard me with admonitions to wait until marriage, but I did envy the clear point on the horizon for switching from "desperately rubbing your junk against another person's nonjunk because that doesn't count for some reason" to "doing regular sex." I'm glad I didn't wait *that* long; saving your virginity for marriage feels as arbitrary as never driving a car until your wedding night. I imagine there's a lot of "Sorry to stop so short!" and "Whoops! I thought I'd fit into that space more smoothly!"

And what does it mean to be "ready"? When leaving my apartment, I've said "I'm ready to go!" and meant everything from "I'm at the front door!" to "I just need to put my shoes on!" to "I am basically still asleep!"

In the context of sexuality, "ready" has an even squishier definition. Does it mean monogamous and in love? At peace with one's own place in the universe? Or just . . . sufficiently horny? Even though I was *definitely* the third thing, I dragged my feet, unclear on what the ideal circumstances even constituted.

To me, the idea of readiness superseded every other sexual concern. Concerns like:

- Did I want to have sex?
  (Yes, definitely.)

- Did people want to have sex with me?
  (Yes, inexplicably.)

- Did I have physical opportunities to have sex?
  (Yes, occasionally.)

- Did I understand how to have sex?
  (**Yes, technically.**)

Through my late adolescence, I worked myself into such a frenzy viewing sex as a "leveling up" experience. I pictured it as the part of a video game where you've made it through a gauntlet of adventures, and you're ready to approach some kind of giant spiky turtle and then, at long last, fuck that turtle (for the sake of this metaphor). I just wanted some reassurance that sex itself would help the relationship progress to the next iteration of dating.

Sex existed as an abstract concept, which of course it was, because I wasn't having it. In fact, I could barely believe that *anyone* was. In late high school, a group of classmates and I went with our significant others to one friend's family lake house. When everyone else showed up late to lunch, I quipped, "Where were you guys? Doing it?" As I met my friends' eyes, I saw that the answer, universally, was *Uhhh, yeah. Duh.* I was stunned. *Aren't you guys afraid of . . . well, everything?* I thought.

The longer I waited, the worse things got. Pressure intensified. My standards for the right moment and the right person escalated. My feelings for one girlfriend had already begun to fade by the time she put an offer explicitly on the table (or, more accurately, "on the extra-long twin bed in her dorm room"), so it would have felt wrong to increase our level of intimacy. Another young woman I dated in college didn't seem to want a long-term relationship, so I felt reluctant to make myself more vulnerable by *losing my virginity* (gasp) to her. I had kissed a few other girls, too (I swear), but making out with someone at a party, or even having a long-running, sporadic hookup with a friend never seemed like the right circumstances for a first time. But in all those situations, either their first times had been in the past or they'd decided I was the right person for them. They were ready! Why wasn't I? I let an undefinable concept of "perfect" become the enemy of, well, maybe not even "good," but *anything at all*.

My concept of sex as a transitional, transformative experience *totally* neglected it as an activity you actually do with your human body. And, like most physical talents, it's something that you have to work at to perfect, and it's not something that comes naturally to me, specifically. I don't know why I assumed that although it had taken me years of practice to shoot a competent free throw, I'd immediately start having spine-tingling, soul-merging sex right away.

Making love is the opposite of learning to drive or skydiving, activities during which you start with another person there and then graduate to doing it on your own. With sex stuff, you start alone, and then add another person later, which makes sense because the danger of falling twenty thousand feet to your death is (usually) minimal when you are masturbating. But knowing how to attend to your own body (at which I had become something of an expert, not to brag) only goes so far when you introduce a partner with her own set of needs and expectations into the mix.

So, inexperience became a mounting impediment[1] as the years went on, in large part because I *hate* being bad at things in front of people, which, I realize, is not a unique quality. Nobody

---

1   Pun intended, and knocked out of the goddamn park.

is like, "Hey watch me fall off this skateboard!" But I hate it more than most people. I'd rather practice something a hundred times in private and then show off a version of it that I think is pretty good before I accept feedback. The aforementioned driver's ed, for example, with an instructor seated next to you, foot on an extra brake pedal, was agony. Just let me noodle around in an empty parking lot, and if I hit something, fail me. I'd rather just be told I'm not good enough once, rather than over and over as I improve by increments.

When I played sports as a kid, I resisted my coaches' real-time input:

"Choke up on that bat!"

"Elbow in!"

"Don't aim! Throw!"

"I know," I'd seethe quietly. "Just let me try it again."

The last piece of advice was always particularly galling. "Don't aim! Throw!" is a pitching maxim, the upshot of which is, "Don't think too hard! Trust your instincts!" By nature, I am not a thrower. I'm an aimer. I think about things. Then I overthink them. And then sometimes, for good measure, I over-overthink them. I distrust my own instincts like they're advice that was whispered to me by a nemesis. *Are you trying to trick me, me?* I wonder.

The upside is, I rarely make rash decisions like getting face tattoos or making massive investments in cryptocurrencies. The downside is, I perform dismally at instinct-based activities like sports and sex, the latter of which is a lot like a team sport that you play with two people (or more than two, I've heard, sometimes, but if you've played it that way, kindly keep it to yourself).

The more I treated my first time like a *thing*, the more of a thing it became. So while I searched for the perfect partner and optimal circumstances, I was unwittingly undermining the relationships I was in by leaving my girlfriends and dates as consistently unfucked as a husband in a 1990s sitcom. ("Come on, Debra! Shhh. The kids are asleep!") And, as we learned from the show *Everybody Loves Raymond—Except His Wife, Who Won't Even Throw Him a Hand Job Every Once in a While*, that takes its toll on a relationship.

Also, I should say for the record, I was doing . . . other stuff. I don't want to get into exactly what constitutes "other stuff," because it's gross to read about what a teenage boy (or, as I thought of myself, a teenage *man*) did with his penis. It was sexual, although it wasn't quite *sex*, and it definitely wasn't *sexy*. Suffice it to say, I was doing stuff I didn't want my parents to know about, but nothing that would really have horrified them. Also for the record: I was not one of those people who "preserved" their virginity for marriage by experimenting with anal sex. (That is a real type of person. According to my observations, they often get married young, presumably to stop having so much anal sex.)

In any case, way after I should have (i.e., in my last months of college), I decided that I'd met the right person. She was smart and funny and pretty and nice. Also, she still is; she hasn't died. She didn't seem to openly or secretly hate me. I didn't fear making myself vulnerable to her. I was ready to level up, but I didn't have the vocabulary. Fortunately, she did.

After a few months of dating, she very maturely was like, "Hey, why aren't we having sex?" And I explained my reasons, and she was very understanding and then we had sex, and it was emotionally very exciting and physically pretty much what you'd expect, and nothing was different afterward except we then had sex more times, which was also fun. Aside from that, though, everything stayed the same. Our relationship hadn't gone to any next level. I didn't have a deeper (*hehe*) understanding of love or humanity. Nothing was transformed in me or her or us. My girlfriend was a human woman, not a cocoon I crawled into as a boy and exited as a man, which is a gross metaphor, but it's as close as I can get to explaining what I'd thought would have happened.

That is, nothing changed while we were together. A few months later, though, we broke up. Of course we did. You don't often stay with the person you lose your virginity to well into adulthood unless you're a character in a Billy Joel song, and even then you still get divorced. One problem with deciding that someone is the "right person," it turns out, is that when she isn't, you end up shaken to the foundation. You lose faith in your own meticulous judgment and your prospects for future happiness. You cry a lot in your car. "You," of course, means me.

I wasn't wronged by our breakup, but I had been *wrong*. Not about whether my girlfriend was the "right person" but about whether any person could bear the burden that I'd saddled her with in my mind. I'd thought I was finally *ready*, but how could I have been when our breakup had left me distraught and lonely? I, probably for the last time in my life, wrote some poetry that I never showed to anyone. It was embarrassing. I was on the wrong side of twenty to be having what was essentially a teenage breakup.

Once I finished grieving (geez, I'm still so melodramatic about this), I finally figured out that there was no significant difference between having had sex and not having had it. I realized that *every* time you have sex is essentially your first time until you figure out what you're doing. If you don't know which way the condom goes on, it's your first time. If you don't bother with foreplay, it's your first time. If you can't locate the clitoris, it is definitively your first time. Obviously these specifics are not applicable for all genders and sexual orientations, but you should probably learn where the clitoris is just from an anatomical/medical standpoint. Unless your bodies lock into an immediate rhythm through a force of fortunate chemistry, every first time with a new partner is a first time with the potential to be as uncomfortable, but also as exciting and special, as your first first time.

I plunged into my twenties having not just teenage feelings but teenage sex as well. I crossed the boundary that had been such a stumbling block for me, but that still left me basically right where I was before. You don't go from virgin to sex genius overnight, in the same way you don't pick up a guitar for the first time and start shredding solos. (Yes, I know that analogy doesn't quite track, considering I spent high school and college shredding sex solos.) I had become infinitely more experienced, statistically speaking, while gaining only marginally more experience. And as withholding as I'd been with past partners, I was equally clumsy and bumbling with women after.

I've spent the last decade figuring out all the niceties of physical intimacy that I assumed my peers had grasped years earlier. At what point do you trust the efficacy of birth control pills and stop using condoms? How fast can you shower after sex without it seeming like a direct insult to the person you've just slept with? How do you know when it's going to be a one-night stand? Sometimes women want you to choke them, even after deciding to sleep with you based on your exceptionally not-chokey personality. What then?

Sex, for me, aside from the fun and excitement and intimacy and pleasure, has always been shot through with trepidation. The part of sex I'd been taught to think of as *sex* was awkward and hard to initiate. And for a long time it was routinely brief, which for the women I was with may have been a mixed blessing, in a "the food was terrible, and such small portions" kind of way. And all that is on top of having what's technically known as "a pretty mediocre dick."

I was jealous not just of people who were great at sex, but of people who were bad at it and fine with that. I don't admire them, but I've always envied the guys who reach sexual climax and go, "GAME OVER! TIME FOR SLEEP!" What a simple, clearheaded existence that must be. I imagine guys like that aggressively sending back overcooked steaks at restaurants and demanding hotel vouchers when their flights are delayed. It's not a life to aspire to, but I can see the appeal of going through life feeling good and feeling good about it, no matter the cost to others, like you're a Republican senator.

Not me, though!

Throughout my adult life, I've always blamed the experience gap for any anxiety or poor performance, but maybe that's not the case. Maybe it's just a thing I'll always be fine but not great at, like parallel parking or sautéing broccoli. And over time, I've gotten less nervous and more competent. I've figured out how to minimize my deficiencies and make up for them with good listening, sincere effort, and, of course, apologizing when I screw up badly. Weirdly, that's also how I got through my time playing youth sports. Because at heart, I'll always be an aimer, not a thrower.

. . . Try, Try Again

Weathering the Tantrums

I worked as a full-time preschool teacher for four years, which came as a surprise, even to me. Part of the shock stemmed from the fact that I didn't go to school for education. Now, that sentence could (accurately) refer to the amount of time I devoted to extra-curriculars instead of homework, but what I meant was: I didn't have formal training to be a teacher. And even if I had, I'm not sure a degree in education would have prepared me for the great-est challenges of the job, like what to do when a student wedges a Cheerio in her nostril, or how to react when a four-year-old hears you curse under your breath.

I graduated with a double major in English and creative writ-ing with a minor in Spanish, so the only thing I'm qualified for is *esto* (that's Spanish for "this"). I knew I wanted to be a writer, but at the time I finished school, that wasn't an immediate option, on the technicality that I had never written anything good enough for someone to pay me for it.

As the end of my final college semester approached, I started scanning online classified ads for a job. Like, any job. Years earlier, my dad had forbidden me from following his footsteps into a career in construction. Of course, my overall lack of physical strength and coordination would have been an impediment as well, so he didn't have much to worry about. *What kind of jobs do people even have?* I wondered.

I revealed my aimlessness to my mom over the phone, and she asked a question that should have occurred to me already.

"Why don't you look for a job teaching preschool? You know you're good at it, and you don't hate it."

Oh, right, duh, I thought. My mother had been the director of a small independent school for the previous twelve years, and ever since I was old enough to have a summer job, I'd worked there as an assistant, dousing squirming toddlers with sunscreen and providing an extra pair of eyes on field trips, in case a restless three-year-old made a break for the otter enclosure at the zoo. Parents get *very* upset if you let otters eat their child, and only slightly less upset if you let their child eat an otter. ("You *know* we are raising Hunter on a plant-based diet!") My last four semesters of college, I'd even worked through the school year as a part-time Spanish teacher for grades kindergarten through eight, a job my yet-to-be-completed Spanish minor left me woefully underqualified for.

As unfit as I was to do my father's job, I was—though I hadn't realized it—incredibly well prepared to follow in my mom's career footsteps. My hours of classroom experience, plus a bachelor's degree, meant I was just a single self-taught community college class away from a head teacher certification, but it hadn't occurred to me that I could teach as a *job* job, partly because it was *fun*. It didn't feel like going to work, the way most people talk about it.

And teachers still seemed so adult to me, so noble and dedicated to the mission of cultivating the minds of young people.

Obviously there were exceptions to that rule. When I was in high school, a substitute teacher named Mr. Burns (a rough name to have so close to the peak of *The Simpsons'* popularity) was fired after sitting idly by while three students pooled thirty-five dollars and paid a fourth student to masturbate into a Dixie cup under his desk. While the firing was clearly justified, he was subbing in a Business 101 class, and those students had provided a vivid, disgusting object lesson in the principle of supply and demand, so . . . was it really that wrong? (It was.)

As we embarked on our young careers, several college friends and I signed a lease on a house in Allston, an outer Boston neighborhood best summed up as "your parents' basement away from your parents' basement." By the time we moved in, I had whipped through my Child Development 101 course at Bunker Hill Community College without ever meeting a professor, and I'd started applying for teaching positions. With employment on the horizon and my Ikea bed frame assembled (with considerable help from my numerous roommates), my adult life seemed to be coming together after all—at least, as much as an adult life can when you have an Ikea bed frame and numerous roommates.

I lined up a few interviews right away. Part of my good luck had to do with the timing. It was a year before the housing crash imploded the economy, so people still had the income to send their kids to private preschool, as well as jobs to go to that made it necessary to hire people to care for their children during the day in the first place.

The other part of my good fortune was sexism, which I realize might require a little more explanation.

When I tell people I used to teach preschool (or mentioned it at the time, even), I get mixed responses. Generally, people without kids recoil, thinking (at best) *Why would you put yourself through that?* or (at worst) *I am definitely talking to a pedophile right now.* People with kids are generally enthusiastic. "That is so important. There are so few men in that field," they often say, although occasionally it carries an undercurrent of, "Of course you spend all day around babies, you giant wimp."

Still, simply being a man (which I technically am, although I think of myself more as a "dude" or a "guy") got my foot in the door. The scarcity of male applicants helped me stand out, request a flexible schedule, and even negotiate a livable, if unspectacular, salary. I guess what I'm saying is, I had the exact experience that men have applying for pretty much every job, and the opposite experience of a woman applying for a position in a male-dominated field. I'm not *proud* of that fact, but I am *aware* of it. And, not to flaunt my privilege, but most of the time, I had the men's bathroom of the church in which our school was housed to myself for the entire day. I could have used it as a storage unit or boutique haberdashery, and nobody would have caught on.

Unlike me, my colleagues were real-deal teachers. Which is to say, they were much more knowledgeable and dedicated and professional and experienced than I was.

Committed early childhood educators don't make as much money as they deserve, but they're so important. Devoted preschool teachers can instill their students with the social and emotional grounding they need to thrive for years to come.

Another, less well-known fact about preschool teachers is that they party like monsters. There's a phenomenon known, possibly problematically, as "teacher Tourette's," in which as soon as teachers are out of earshot of their students, they'll immediately start cursing like a mob lawyer on the phone with a loan shark. Not to mention the drinking. On a few occasions, a group of teachers from my school came to see me do stand-up, and they were reliably the rowdiest table in the club. It was like performing for a bachelorette party with no bachelorette. Once I did a show at a rehab center a few blocks from our school, and a coworker whom I will not identify smuggled in booze in a Dunkin' Donuts cup. I was amazed at her hard work and tenderness with the kids day after day, especially since every time I saw her at night, I would think, *I sure hope you get home okay.*

I was less of a partyer, but after late nights at shows or hanging out with friends, I would wear a shirt and tie to work the next morning to trick people into thinking I was put together. "You look so nice today," my boss would tell me. I'd thank her and then return to counting down the minutes until I could spend my lunch break in my car, napping in the driver's seat.

Because I wasn't crafty or organized, I tried to find other ways to make myself valuable in the classroom, mostly to avoid being revealed as dead weight. My coworkers excelled at the *teaching* part of teaching, so I needed to carve out my own niche, which was tricky because *teaching* was the entire job. My first plan was to introduce Spanish lessons into our classroom. I'd never taught Spanish to kids quite this young before, but the beauty of teaching any specific skill to four-year-olds is that nobody expects them to learn that much. If they can count to twenty and pick up the words for enough body parts to play Simon Says in another language, their parents will do cartwheels with glee.

I also learned that while the school held a yearly holiday party in December and a graduation ceremony in June, there was no real performance element for the children. This seemed like an opportunity for me to inject some of my expertise into the job. My expertise, at the time, consisted primarily of pretending I had expertise. I took the initiative and wrote a holiday play (a non-denominational "'Twas the Night Before Christmas" parody) and rehearsed it with my students a few afternoons every week leading up to the party. This served the dual purposes of getting the kids ready to go onstage and avoiding learning how to make caterpillars out of egg cartons and other things that better teachers do.

Over my years in the classroom, I came up with a simple formula for writing a children's performance. Number one: Make sure an adult narrator is doing all the talking. Write the dialogue in a way that describes the action for the audience and literally tells the performers what they should be doing at every moment. ("All the snowmen and snowwomen became very sleepy . . . even Lucas.") Number two: Throw in a few songs. Just the hits. "Itsy Bitsy Spider," "This Old Man," stuff like that. No need to get fancy and try to teach them a Beatles tune. Nobody cares how good your taste in music is. This is all about how few of the children start crying and run offstage. (Anything less than 20 percent attrition is a major success.) Finally: Keep it short. No need to draw this thing out. It's not *Angels in America*. And even if it was, it would be a shitty version of *Angels in America* because four-year-olds are bad at acting. You want to get in and get out before all the younger siblings get bored and start running full speed into each other. Nothing derails a holiday party like a toddler with a concussion.

The play, as rudimentary as it was, was a hit. It turned out that I was moderately skilled at *something*. I wasn't dead weight in the classroom. I was more like . . . I don't know . . . regular weight.

My other special skill, I came to realize, was listening to children cry. In most cases, stoically sitting through a child's emotional outburst makes you what people might call "a heartless monster" or "an actual sociopath." As a preschool teacher, though, it's part of the job. Kids are going to cry. Most of the time, there's nothing you can do to stop them. (The exception to that rule being if you spot a child within two seconds of them falling on the ground or running right into another kid's face, you can sometimes trick them with a swift, convincing counternarrative: "You're okay! Don't worry about it. Those were just your baby teeth anyway.") So you have to get good at weathering the tears. Not to brag, but I was *very* good at sitting calmly beside crying children.

At age four, children have the skills to articulate *why* they're unhappy ("I don't *wanna go inside yet!*"), but even after they identify the problem, they don't have the wherewithal to keep from melting down like an ice sculpture in front of a space heater. Just about anything can set them off: skipping their regular nap, sleeping for too long, being told they have to finish their lunch, running out of lunch to eat, their best friend not wanting to play with them, their best friend wanting to play with the same toy as them. Literally any stimulus can provide the inspiration for a truly seismic fit of histrionics. If you're not around kids often, you might not know that Johnson & Johnson's "No More Tears" shampoo doesn't just refer to the product's gentle formulation. It's also a silent prayer that parents and childcare providers utter at least once a day. "Please. No more tears. I can't take it."

I spent at least thirty minutes every day on the floor next to a child in the throes of a full-on tantrum (the child's tantrum, not mine). Children cried. They screamed. In some cases they tore at their clothes and pounded the floor like tiny, inconsolable war widows. They couldn't be reasoned with, and in some cases they couldn't even be comforted. So I sat beside them, offering words of encouragement in my most soothing tone. "I know," I'd say. "Life can be really hard sometimes. It's so hard not to get what you want. I've been there, too. But I'm sure if you take some deep breaths and relax your body, you'll get a turn with that green marker very soon. I fully understand that none of the other identical green markers will suffice. It's important to have standards."

My coteachers marveled at my placid stamina.

"I don't know how you do that," a colleague once remarked, after watching me weather a forty-minute-long tsunami of tears.

To be honest, I wasn't sure, either. Some of it I chalked up to my natural disposition. But also, as a straight guy in your twenties, you get used to people crying angrily at you. You're just not good enough at relationships to avoid it. The other teachers, mostly heterosexual women, would have had the upper hand dealing with a stoic child who "just doesn't want to fucking talk about it, okay, Jennifer?"

I'd fallen into my job, but I ended up loving it. Even on the most exhausting days, something sweet and nice usually happened, too. I got to see kids hit developmental milestones, form lasting friendships, and be at least intermittently charming and hilarious.

Some highlights:

- One of the sweetest kids I ever taught was a small tornado of a girl named Della. Her hands were always sticky, and by noon every day, her hair was matted down to her head from sweat and who knows what other thickening agent, with several strands having found their way into her mouth. She had the worst gross motor skills I'd ever seen. She walked too fast, as if she were constantly finding herself on an unexpected downhill slope. She fell over *all the time*, and she'd often run to hug me at top speed, resulting in an inadvertent head-butt to my groin. At lunch time, we'd have the students pour their own milk and water from little pitchers, for dexterity. Della spilled an entire pitcher basically every day, causing the other kids (and some teachers) to sigh with exasperation. Once a week or so, she poured herself a Dixie cup of milk without any collateral damage, and holding my breath while watching her in those moments felt like witnessing a successful heart transplant.

- Once, right at the end of the school day, all the kids were signing their names on a big group project. Most of the class had pretty sloppy handwriting, but almost all of them could write their names from start to finish. One kid hadn't quite figured it out. He'd write his initials or just a big illegible squiggle, like the world's tiniest doctor signing off on a prescription pad. But this time, he hit the first letter and kept his focus straight through the second one. The other kids had finished and were getting antsy to move on to our next activity. "No need to rush," I said to the class, "we've got plenty of time." Really I just wanted to avoid putting a spotlight on this one kid. It took him two full minutes to write out the four letters in his first name, and he walked away from the table with a slight, proud smile like an NBA player who just iced a playoff game with a pair of clutch free throws. There is no way he remembers that afternoon as vividly as I do.

• At lunch one day, the girls in the class started to tease a boy named Liam. "Marry me!" they jeered. "Marry me! No not her! Marry me, Liam, me!" Liam became visibly flustered. (Of course he did. No one had ever proposed to him before.) "You have to choose who you're going to marry or time's going to run out and you'll be left without anyone to marry at all." Finally, Liam couldn't take it anymore. "I'm sorry, girls, but I'm going to marry Owen." We all turned to look at Owen, who had his arms crossed and was nodding deeply in the affirmative. It was very heartwarming. The girls protested, but when Liam held firm in his decision, and I assured them it was not against the rules for a boy to marry another boy, they accepted his choice. It felt, in that moment, like maybe people *are* inherently good, and maybe prejudice is learned and can be unlearned. And then I remembered that I was dealing with a sample size of fifteen people, none of whom even knew their parents' first names. So while the conversation gave me reason to hope, it was not exactly a watershed moment in American culture.

Days like those made me feel, if not important, at least useful. I left school every day physically tired but excited to head home and work on writing or do stand-up sets. I never felt like I'd *wasted* my time, either. Work just felt like a slightly different, but also productive, use of my day. Plus, because I thought of teaching as a job and not a career, I didn't stress out too badly about my long-term financial stability; only in the few months before I left did I really start thinking about my scant down-the-line prospects for owning a home or (*gasp*) retiring. Not that my long-term career goal of "comedian and writer" would guarantee a life free of roommates and laundry done at my parents' house, either.

As my tenure as a teacher extended, I realized that I *did* bring something to the table as an educator. The patience I was able to show to sobbing kids relieved the emotional burden on my coteachers, who were already displaying maximum empathy to the groups of little boys who would have gladly spent their mornings hitting each other in the face with toy trains and wooden blocks. And the storytelling and improv games we played exercised different creative muscles than the visual and tactile art projects that the other teachers designed so expertly. Not to mention that the pride (and some fear) in the students' faces when they put on our Totally Nondenominational but Still Kind of Christmasy holiday play was genuine and exhilarating to witness. Kids who never thought they'd be able to stand onstage looked out into the crowd and sang their hearts out (or, on occasion, just waved nervously to their parents, but that's not nothing).

What I thought was laziness was actually an application of my skill set for the benefit of the kids (with a little legitimate laziness mixed in). What was really important, I realized, was staying engaged with the kids all day, meeting them on their level, not assuming what they needed from me, and giving them outlets to play and grow.

When I quit my job to move to New York, my coteachers had each of our students illustrate a page of a book that they put together for me. When they handed it to me, I cried a little, which was something I wasn't used to at all.

The Thanksgiving Dragon

There are really only two kinds of mistakes: the kind where you did your best and fell short, and the kind where you should have known better but you messed up anyway. The first kind of screwup is more common and easier to let go of, and the second kind is (hopefully) rarer, but it sticks with you.

Often as a teacher, you end up in situations that you can't prepare for, and you can't always fake your way through them. Once I was sitting cross-legged in a circle of probably fifteen three-to-five-year-olds, when I heard our classroom assistant hurrying over from across the room. She leaned down and whispered in my ear. I sighed as I turned to face the kids. My coteachers had left for the day. I was in charge. This was my problem.

"Nobody's in trouble," I began, "but did anyone here accidentally poop on the floor in the middle of the classroom?"

Not a single child responded.

"Okay, let me put it this way: *Someone* pooped on the floor. If it was you, it's okay. You can tell me, and we can get you cleaned up."

Still no one moved. It was as if the kids had conspired to

conceal the floor pooper's identity, like they had spontaneously developed the concept of omertà, the mafia code of silence. More likely, they knew who had done the pooping but refused to rat him or her out because of a feeling of vicarious embarrassment. *There but for the grace of god poop I.* Whatever the reason, they decided to stonewall me. That's the thing about children that age: if you need them to tell you something, they clam up, and when you want a moment of quiet, they ramble on indefinitely, like a Bob Dylan song with six verses.

Issues like this cropped up just about every day during my tenure as a pre-K teacher. At least this one wasn't completely foreign to me. During my freshman year in college, a mystery student we knew only as the Phantom Shitter defecated in a shower stall once a week, so I had some experience solving this kind of mystery. At last, I was putting my degree to use.

In my years of teaching, I only really screwed up one time in a way that I regret. There was a student whom I should have been there for, and I let him down. I think about it all the time.

One morning in early November of my second year of teaching, Sean, a student I liked very much, ran by me on the playground wearing a bright green winter hat with a fake lizard tail on the back, complete with plush yellow spikes and plates. (Author's note: You are not *supposed* to have favorite students, but every teacher does. To not have favorites would require a level of patience and detachment you usually find only in Buddhist monks or coma patients.) Sean had a big, round face and always seemed to be in a good mood, like Charlie Brown without the anxiety. I waved to him, and he slowed down, bursts of sand kicking up in front of him.

"Hey, bud," I said. "I love the Stegosaurus hat."

Sean furrowed his brow, confused. He never seemed unhappy when confronted with an obstacle, just genially perplexed. "It's not a Stegosaurus," he replied.

I didn't feel bad for assuming it was a dinosaur. Pretty much everything a four-year-old boy expresses interest in is either a dinosaur or an anthropomorphic motor vehicle. "Oh, I'm sorry," I said. "What is it then?"

Sean's big circle face furrowed with resolve, his features scrunching together and convening at his nose.

"This year," he said, giving each word as much gravity as possible from someone who is three feet tall with a slight speech impediment and still believes that Santa Claus is real, "for Thanksgiving . . . I'm going to be a dragon."

Now *I* was confused. Thanksgiving celebrations, as far as I knew, rarely called for costumes, and even in the event of some kind of pageant, few if any retellings of the Pilgrims' arrival in (and forcible takeover of) North America included a large fire-breathing serpent. Where could he possibly have come up with this idea?

But then I realized: Halloween was only a week before. And when you're four years old, you probably don't have a super-clear memory of holidays you've celebrated in the past. Sean must have dressed up for Halloween and formed an association in his brain: "holidays = costumes." It wasn't *that* reckless a leap of logic. Plus, what a delightful, whimsical world it would be if every Presidents' Day, the streets were full of kids dressed as Abraham Lincoln and Optimus Prime.

"That sounds like a great idea," I said with a smile. Honestly, I didn't know if it was a great idea, but it felt too cruel to destroy the exciting future he'd created in his mind. Plus, it was funny to me to imagine a little kid at the dinner table, fully costumed as a dragon while his entire family wore Dockers and button-down shirts. Sean grinned and took off at top speed across the playground.

Over the next few weeks, I'd check in with Sean on the status of his outfit from time to time. "How's the costume coming along?" I'd ask. He'd usually just nod and let out a furtive giggle, unable to contain his excitement for (presumably) the anniversary of the *Mayflower* landing on Plymouth Rock and its passengers dressing up in bearskins and going wigwam to wigwam, begging for candy. Again, he wouldn't have been that far off. The colonists received the treat of a wide swath of the North American continent from sea to shining sea. The trick they played was, in essence, genocide. But, much like with the costume thing, I was not ready to say that out loud and shatter a child's world.

The Wednesday before Thanksgiving, we had a half day at school, and when the parents came to scoop their kids up after lunch, Sean's mother took me aside. Her voice was quiet, and her tone betrayed a slight dismay.

"So, for the past month or so, Sean has been telling us that he's going to be a dragon for Thanksgiving. We keep telling him that Thanksgiving isn't a costume holiday, but he's *very* excited about it. Do you have any idea why he thinks that?" Her face bore a look of genuine puzzlement, not unlike her son when I asked him about his Stegosaurus [*sic*] hat.

"Dr. Hyden, I have no idea," I lied, right to her face, while looking her dead in the eyes. Why do they make eye contact seem like such a big deal in the movies? It's not any harder than lying while gazing off in the distance, and it's way more effective. In my defense, the costume hadn't been my idea, and what difference did it make if she knew I'd been hyping Sean up for the past few weeks? It's not like there was anything I could do about it at that point.

In the opposite of my defense, I was now even more curious to hear what the Hyden family Thanksgiving dinner was like.

The following Monday, I returned to work eager for news. Normally after a long weekend, you ask the kids to share how they spent their time off, and you get a mixture of total forgetfulness, long-winded (and often unrelated) anecdotes, and total fabrication. It's a charming but not especially illuminating conversation. This time, though, I couldn't wait to hear one specific story.

Just after drop-off, I approached Sean by the cubby where he hung his coat. "How was your holiday?" I asked.

"Good," he said, grinning per usual. He was playing hardball. I'd have to be more direct.

"Okay," I replied, "but how did your costume go over?"

"Ugh," he sighed, his face falling, *"you don't dress up for Thanksgiving!"* It was the first time I'd ever seen him so unhappy, and possibly the first feeling of "how could I have been such a rube?" he'd experienced in his young life. And it was all my fault. I'd hung him out to dry. By sparing his feelings up front and encouraging his imagination, I had led him up an emotional cliff from which the only way down was a free fall.

As a teacher, sometimes you make a genuine positive difference in a child's life, and other times, well . . . other times, you shit the floor.

Some Things That I, a Childcare Professional, Was Professionally Obligated to Say to Kids

"Yes, it is hard to ride a unicycle."

"Please eat your lunch with your *mouth*."

"I can tell you're not napping because you just told me, 'I'm napping.'"

"Maybe your friends will want to play with you if you stop hitting them."

"It's okay. The shark in the book is a *nice* shark, and he's not even a *real* shark."

"I guess, since you are already sitting in the urinal, just let me know when you're done peeing so I can help you down."

"Yes, I know you wish your mommy was here to pick you up right now. Trust me. I want that, too."

Good Deeds, Unrewarded

Much like the sex education I got in high school, the lessons on drugs and alcohol I received there scared me off of trying a generally fun thing by instilling me with worst-case-scenario panic. My anxiety-based sobriety meant that, for years, I was almost always the designated driver. And there is no good deed that is rewarded less richly and punished more frequently than designated driving.[1]

As a nondrinking car-haver, I did a lot of designated driving for friends and roommates from late high school through the first few years after college. Somebody had to do it, after all, and I was already going to be there. What was I going to do, *not* drive my roommates home from the party or bar or friend's house or woods or abandoned summer camp? That would have seemed a little spiteful of me. "Sorry, guys! Gotta drive this empty car home! See you back at the house later tonight! And enjoy the drunk scavenger hunt that gets you there!"

---

1   The only upside, as far as I can tell, is that your friends are less likely to die, which I admit is a significant perk.

It's not fun to be the person buckling his friend into the passenger seat, fearing that, cocky and limber from tequila shots, he might attempt a Tom Cruise–type tuck-and-roll out of the moving vehicle. (Or, even more alarming, a Tom Cruise–type late-night conversion to Scientology.)

When you agree to drive for the night, you're admitting that, at some point, your evening will get less enjoyable.[2] Unless you are going out to a club and feel comfortable hitting the dance floor sober (I don't know how that could be possible; maybe you are a trained ballerina or something), the sloppier your friends get, the harder they get to be around. Especially because there comes a time in the night when you're not just the driver. You're also the pizza delivery guy, bodyguard, babysitter, therapist, and cleaning crew.

The worst part is, as your friends' inhibitions decline, all those tasks become trickier, and even if the scene gets real messy, you're not allowed to leave. That's when you become *most* necessary. You're the fixer, like Harvey Keitel in that scene from *Pulp Fiction* in which Quentin Tarantino seems weirdly comfortable using the N-word. So instead of getting to pull an Irish goodbye (a quiet,

---

2 Don't get me wrong, there are *lots* of ways to have fun without drinking, but none of them are predicated on serving as the unpaid chauffeur for a car full of people whose plan for the night *starts* with the premise "No matter where the night takes us, the one thing we know for sure is that at the end of it we will be too impaired to drive." That means the absolute ceiling for your friends' cognitive capacity as the evening winds down will be "should not get behind the wheel." And the floor sits somewhere around "human-size bag of wet cement, able to answer questions only by moaning."

unannounced exit), you are basically stuck packing an in-progress Irish wake into your car. Everyone's drunk and there's a lot of shouting and crying and hugging and punching.

Just kidding: the worst part is when people puke in your car.

Because I am a good friend, I designated-drove enough that *several* people puked in my car. Someone from my college improv team barfed in my back seat on the way back to campus from a show in Boston's North End. On a trip to visit a professor over the summer after my junior year at Brandeis, a friend vomited out the window of a car I was driving, just as we passed the mini golf course where she'd had her first kiss years earlier.[3] She wasn't even drunk; she was hungover from drinking the previous night. I've never seen a more apt metaphor for "you're not as young as you used to be" before or since. The chaos didn't end when I graduated, either. Years after I finished college, my long-distance girlfriend came to visit for my twenty-sixth birthday and threw up by her feet as she rode shotgun on the way home from my party.

Even when friends weren't actively soiling the already-shabby cloth interior of my used Toyota Corolla, my need to be the one in control made me stress out while everyone else was at their most relaxed. During the doldrums after our senior-year finals but before graduation, two buddies (let's call them Len and Devin because those names rhyme with their real names) asked me for a ride to Providence, Rhode Island, to see an art exhibition that Alison, a friend of theirs from home, was putting on. A quick day-trip

---

3 It wasn't *my* car, but I was driving it because no one else was in any condition to.

felt like just the right way to break up the "not a girl, not yet a woman" week between the cocoon of college and my entry into the "real world," where I'd be as fresh and unemployable as a butterfly.

Before we left campus, Len and Devin split a pot brownie between the two of them.

A quick thing here: not to sound old, but nowadays, you can get specifically dosed weed edibles at retail outlets or from doctors who stopped wanting to work hard in many US states. They're potent and professionally made and their active ingredient is spread out uniformly, like the cream in the center of an Oreo cookie. But back in the dark ages of 2007, you had to get marijuana-infused baked goods from, like, just some guy. So when you ate a brownie, each bite could potentially be no drugs or all of the drugs. And there was no way to know which had happened for at least half an hour. The strategy for consuming weed edibles since time immemorial has been: Eat not nearly enough. Wait a few minutes while nothing happens. EAT WAY TOO MUCH.

Len and Devin climbed into my car, where Len, still convinced the drugs hadn't really taken hold yet, fell asleep in the back seat so fast I was surprised he managed to buckle his seat belt. This was only a problem because he was supposed to be navigating. Devin was holding it together surprisingly well, by which I mean he stayed conscious for the entire ninety-minute trip.

I hoped a little rest would help Len push through the "too high" phase of his brownie, but it had just the opposite effect. When we arrived in Providence, he could barely speak. He needed help getting out of the car, and once we pulled him out onto the sidewalk, he stood still, unsteady and nervous, like a baby standing upright for the first time without anything to grab on to. He reached his arms out, grasping. I extended my hand, and Len grabbed it. He held on tight for fear of falling, and together we walked slowly down Thayer Street. If you saw us from afar, you would have assumed we were a sweet, elderly couple.

We arrived at Alison's apartment to find her *intensely* un-amused. "What is wrong with him?" she asked.

"He's way too high," we explained.

"Well, he has to go. You have to take him away."

"But we want to see your exhibit," we protested.

"No," she said firmly. "You have to leave."

So, fifteen minutes after we'd parked in downtown Providence, it was decreed that Len was too high for the state of Rhode Island, so we turned around and left. Devin and I helped him back to the car, and we plodded back to school through rush-hour traffic without having seen any art. I'd somehow experienced all the responsibility of giving my impaired friends a ride without any of the fun of being at a party. It was the purest, most annoying version of designated driving.

It's probably not unrelated that two days later I got drunk for the first time.

The night before graduation, I bellied up to the kitchen table for a team beer-drinking competition, my apartment against our downstairs neighbors. We'd orchestrated a weeklong "House Olympics" competition, and this was the final event. My roommates asked me to participate so that we'd have even numbers, and in doing so, they appealed to my one instinct stronger than my fear of losing control: my sense of obligation. We were in a safe space, and I was barely drinking more than the legal limit for being on the road. And it was more for the good of the group. It was basically the designated driving of drinking.

It was on. When the dust settled (we had a very dirty apartment), our side had lost, and I had, predictably, been the one who dragged us down. But I'd made a commitment, so I stayed in my seat until I'd finished all four cans, even though the contest had already been decided. As a novice beer drinker, I struggled to gulp down all forty-eight ounces of Bud Light while it was still cold enough that I didn't have to taste it.[4] As the beer warmed to room temperature, I drank slower and slower. This effect created a vicious cycle whereby it took me so long to finish that I never achieved more than a very slight buzz.

Still, I took the opportunity to engage in another venerated college tradition for the first time: drunk texting. I fired off messages to as many childhood friends as I could think of, most of whom were impressed that I'd gotten wasted (or at least . . . disheveled) but disappointed I'd done it without them. I stayed up late into the night exchanging giddy texts with old friends, partly because of the endorphin rush and partly because I had a Motorola flip phone at the time, so texting took longer than it does now. Once again, not

---

4   More than ten years after that night, I feel comfortable saying this: beer is not good. The better the beer, the worse the beer. Pabst Blue Ribbon is essentially Great Lakes water in a can, so it's fine to drink if you're at a barbecue or trying to get wasted enough to enjoy country music to its full potential. But every craft IPA I've ever had has tasted like gasoline filtered through potting soil. Craft beer tastes like cold brew coffee's hippie cousin who lives in the woods outside Portland. Drinking a beer is a toll you pay for being drunk, and hangovers are the cost of maintenance after the trip.

to sound old, but: kids today with their predictive text have no idea the hell we went through in the early aughts! There was a time where to type an uppercase C you had to hit the 2 key half a dozen times! Show some respect, whippersnappers!

Regardless of whether my goodwill was psychosomatic, I loved the sensation of free-flowing enthusiasm, and I hated how much I loved it. I was the sober friend, the sensible one. Once the novelty of "Josh is drunk for the first/second/third time" wore off, drinking would just be something I did. I'd be simply another person who went out and had fun, just like everyone else. What a nightmare that would be. Even at peak inebriation, I didn't say or do anything ridiculous; I mostly told everyone I'd ever met that I loved them, which I probably did only because that's what people do in the movies after several beers with friends. And they, generously, allowed me to puke feelings into the cars of their lives.

I still drank infrequently for years after that. As long as I lived in Boston, I kept driving my friends around, unwilling to give up full control of my nights but a little looser with my command over my faculties, especially in safe circumstances. I'd have a couple of beverages at a wedding or maybe one at a party we were throwing wherever I was living at the time, as long as I could be mathematically certain I'd be sober when it was time to leave.

When I was twenty-six, I moved to Manhattan, where no one drives, so no one ever asked for a ride. The public transit runs all night, and taxis cluster along the most populous streets like swarms of bees. Sometimes I have three or four drinks, just for fun, and out of courtesy to the city's cab drivers and train conductors, I've never thrown up before I arrive at home.

Have Fun

"Have fun," my friend Myq Kaplan[1] used to say when it was my turn to perform at the open mic at Dick Doherty's Beantown Comedy Vault, which remains, a decade and a half later, the comedy club with the most cumbersome name I've ever heard. It was good advice, and like most good advice, it seemed hard to put into practice, so I didn't.

I was nineteen years old and brand new to stand-up. Myq was a few years older and was already a working comic, which was the only goal in comedy I felt comfortable aspiring to. I'd never met anyone who had a stand-up special or wrote for a sitcom. But Myq got paid to tell jokes, which seemed both exciting and eventually possible for me, too. He emceed at the clubs around Boston and, in fact, performed basically anywhere in New England with a stage: Elks lodges, folk music venues, Chinese restaurants. Myq's act was heavy on rapid-fire wordplay, and the smart, dense jokes stood out at open mics, where a substantial portion of the

---

1 Pronounced "Mike Kaplan."

entertainment sounded like the introductory speeches at a support group for young men who are addicted to masturbating.

I always appreciated Myq's advice; it was nice to have someone be nice to me. Not that the other comedians were cruel. Most of them barely paid attention to me. I eventually made friends with some of the newer comics, but at first we were all too wrapped up in our own neuroses to engage with one another. We buried our heads in our notebooks backstage, slyly watching each other's sets, but not confident enough to compliment each other on a job well done for fear of seeming uncool, or worse, overeager.

The more established comics, stopping by to try out a few minutes of new jokes, didn't seem to notice us at all. Before and after their sets they hung out at the back of the bar upstairs from the basement showroom, talking among themselves and drinking bottles of Michelob Ultra for some reason.

I would have welcomed any attention, even the negative kind. A little trash talk would really have put me at ease. Not a withering critique, just the kind of shit you talk to your friends' faces because they know you don't *really* mean it. It's much better than being bad-mouthed behind your back (although that can still happen in these cases, too) or being ignored entirely.

There's an apocryphal Boston comedy story I've heard for years in which a headliner goes up to his opening act and says, "Look, man. I'll give you twenty bucks if you go out there and just eat it for the whole fifteen minutes. Crickets. No laughs. A total bomb." The opener rolls his eyes and goes out, where he has a fine set to a decent audience response. After fifteen minutes he gets offstage to see the headliner, mouth agape, twenty-dollar bill in hand. "I didn't think you'd really do it," he says, palming the bill to the opener.

I wanted that so bad, the whimsical cruelty of "we all belong here."

Years later, I was backstage waiting to perform my first stand-up set on national television on *Conan*. I chatted with friends and picked at a veggie plate. I was pacing the greenroom, propelled by nervous energy, when Conan O'Brien (the titular Conan) came through the doorway.

"It's so nice to meet you," I said. "Thanks for having me on your show."

"Well, that's not a done deal yet," he said, his face stern. I laughed. It was the most comforting thing I could have heard. For Conan to come backstage and make fun of me right away sent a clear message: "I think you can hang."

Still, absent that, I remained grateful for Myq's consistent kindness and unwavering advice. It was never "have a great set" or even its superstitious backstage surrogate, "break a leg." Every time I was about to take the stage he'd say, "Are you up next? Have fun!" That was my comedy North Star, the effort to enjoy myself. And the fact that someone had taken the time to give me any kind of sincere feedback was almost as good as being made fun of. Without Myq's input, I don't know if I ever would have gotten comfortable.

But for my first year doing stand-up, I was unable to take his simple direction. When I was onstage, having fun never entered my mind.[2] If Myq hadn't mentioned it, I wouldn't have even con-

---

2   If you feel inclined to heckle my book, now would be a good time to drunk-
    enly yell, "Fun didn't enter the audience's mind, either!"

sidered the idea of fun. I didn't get into comedy because it was *fun*.
I did it because it was *exciting*.

I first performed at the Vault the summer between my freshman and sophomore years at college. It was an easy commute, only
a twentyish-minute drive from my parents' house. But when I got
back to school in the fall, the trip became much more difficult.
First, I had to remember to call the club booker on Tuesday to
secure a spot the following Sunday. Then, that Sunday at seven
I'd hop on the free shuttle bus that the Brandeis administration
ran over the weekend so the student body didn't get stir crazy and
turn the campus into the hotel from *The Shining*. I got off the
bus in Harvard Square and took the subway the rest of the way
downtown.

I also had to drag two paid audience members with me in
order to secure my spot onstage. It's what's called a "bringer show,"
which is a club's way of wringing a cover charge out of audience
members who are about to see a show that's not really worth paying for. Usually I brought friends from Brandeis. When I couldn't
entice any of my classmates into the city, I'd desperately try to con
friends who went to college downtown to come to the show. On a
few especially dire nights, I begged my dad and sister to drive into
the city and cough up the seven-dollar entry fee.

Most weeks, as soon as my set ended I collected my things
(notebook, pen, iPod) and ran out the door to catch the last free
shuttle bus back to campus. This wasn't a paid gig, so I was already
losing money on the night. And if I had to take the commuter rail
back from Cambridge to Waltham, it doubled the amount of cash
I'd have to spend on travel.

And while all that was a thrill, it wasn't exactly *fun*. It was new and interesting and stressful and satisfying. But it wasn't really a good time. As much as I enjoyed learning a new skill, I hated that I couldn't get better faster, and the times onstage when the laughs wouldn't come felt acutely unpleasant.

I had to find the excitement in the little things because, on its face, the open mic scene in Boston in the early aughts was not exactly glamorous. Though there were other shows around the city, I mostly stuck to the Vault, a seventy-seat club in the theater district, named because it was housed in the basement of an old bank. The greenroom was behind the literal vault's circular doorway. A twelve-inch-thick reinforced steel door sat perpetually open in the showroom, held ajar by the table farthest from the stage. The weirdness of the room was offset by the smothering normalcy of Remington's, the bar upstairs that the club rented space from.

Remington's was the kind of place where you could guess the entire menu before you saw it. In fact, the bar itself had the same cozy level of "don't think too hard about what's in this" as a loaded potato skin. And they had Stella Artois on tap, but someone would undoubtedly make fun of your fancy European airs if you ordered one. It was kind of like Cheers, but (ironically, considering the business downstairs) the patrons were less funny. By the time the open mic started on Sundays at nine, it was never that crowded.

For months I was too nervous to speak above a squeaky whisper onstage. Even now the energy of my stand-up act is only as electric as what you might generate by rubbing an inflated balloon against a carpet. Back then it was practically a short circuit.

The comedy part of comedy was a science experiment for me back then. Can I make the crowd laugh at a thing I thought of? And if so, could I make another crowd laugh at it the next week? If an experiment isn't replicable, after all, it isn't valid.

The excitement in my first year of comedy didn't come from anything going particularly well. It came from the knowledge of how badly things could go on any given night. The quality of an open mic has a claustrophobically low ceiling and an ear-poppingly low floor. And when you're starting out in comedy, performing is a lot like skydiving,[3] in that the best-case scenario is that you avoid the worst possible outcome, and you walk away living life exactly as you did before.

And given the amount of legwork it took just to get onstage, a bad set felt extra bad. After all, there's nothing like bombing in front of your family after conning them into leaving the house on a Sunday night to make them say, "Don't you have homework you could be doing?"

After several months, though, the shows began to feel more routine. The other comics' faces were more familiar, my own nerves less pronounced. I was getting better, for sure. But I was in an uncanny valley where I had gotten consistent enough that I didn't feel energized by the possibility of failure, but I didn't know how else to enjoy myself. On nights when the excitement wasn't there, I'd manufacture it. I paced before my set. I played loud music in my headphones backstage to try to coax out the adrenaline. Sometimes it worked, and other times it didn't. But I didn't realize

---

3   A lot of things are like skydiving, it turns out!

I'd strayed off course. I'd been ignoring the only real advice I'd ever received. *Have fun.*

My reminder came from an unlikely source. Tom, who is now a good friend of mine, was one of the most intimidating working comedians at the Vault. He was skinny and smoked cigarettes in front of the club and had a cutting sense of humor. If you passed him as you came offstage he'd often tell you, "Good set" and then, after a pause, "Eh. I didn't watch." It wouldn't have felt so bad if he wasn't so funny. His act was *very* dirty and *very* mean. He was still finding his voice, but when his jokes hit, they struck the audience like a sledgehammer.

One night, I was sitting in the lowercase vault in the upper-case Vault going over some notes I'd written for myself. Tom came down the bar's back stairs and walked over to me.

"Are you a comic?" Tom asked. I sat up straight in the booth, proud to have been recognized as a small part of the humble tapestry of the local comedy scene.

"Yeah!" I said, with disproportionate enthusiasm.

"Then give me a pen," he demanded.

The back of my neck tingled with embarrassment. I'd walked right into his sucker punch. I handed over my pen, and Tom walked away with it. As he left, I smiled, realizing I had been recognized after all. *Oh, right*, I thought. *This is supposed to be fun.*

The Blank Postcard

Most people become less exciting as they age, retiring from parties and extreme sports. I have become slightly more fun as I've gotten older, but only incrementally, and the bar was set pretty low to start with.

When I was twenty-five, I started a long-distance relationship with Leah, a younger woman who didn't want to be anyone's girlfriend at all. She was twenty-two, just out of college, and vibrating with ambition. Leah was small with big, wide eyes, which earned people's trust, and a smart, vengeful brain that would destroy them if she felt they had underestimated her. She was a talented writer, and as soon as she'd finished school, she moved to Manhattan, where she worked in media like the protagonist of an HBO prestige comedy. I was still teaching preschool and doing stand-up around Boston, where we'd met.

I visited Leah at her New York apartment that August, and that night she said both "I don't see myself having a boyfriend right now" and "This doesn't have to be a whole big thing, right?" Her explicit reluctance to be in a relationship was, in retrospect, the first sign that maybe we shouldn't have been in a relationship. But despite the two hundred miles between us and Leah's constant insistence that she was a wild stallion (or . . . mare?) who could not be tamed, things continued to get more serious. We texted every day. We spent hours on the phone. One of us visited the other at least twice a month. That's only a casual relationship if you're talking about your conjoined twin.

By December, it was time for the ceremonial Meeting of the Friends. On account of the distance, Leah hadn't had many opportunities to submit me before her friend group as Boyfriend Material. It was decided that on New Year's Eve, I would visit her in New York, where I would tag along on a Girls' Night Out. So the Girls' Night Out signal was sent into the air (a group email chain), and I steeled myself for an evening of high-impact bonding with a Voltron of childhood friends, high school friends, college friends, high school friends' best college friends, and college friends' high school best friends.

But as December 31 drew closer, the Girls' Night Out gaggle began to dwindle. A last-minute trip out of town popped up here. A boyfriend surprised someone with restaurant reservations there. Somehow, New Year's Eve had managed to become a disappointment before it even started, which even for New Year's Eve must represent some sort of record.

I did feel relieved to have avoided such a high-stakes night of socializing. But part of me worried that if I never became enmeshed with Leah's larger social group, I was more likely to be dumped. Determined to create enough fun memories to keep the relationship moving forward, I suggested we get tickets to a show the Roots (my favorite live band) were playing in Brooklyn. The only tickets left were on Craigslist, which meant they could have been legit, counterfeit, or a trick to bring strangers close enough to murder them. Leah, the intrepid Manhattanite, met the seller in person, remaining mercifully unmurdered throughout the transaction.

Our plans had, in my opinion, taken a turn for the better. Then Leah suggested a wrinkle to our evening, and her proposal consisted of the only New Year's celebration more daunting than a Girls' Night Out.

"On New Year's Eve, I think we should do molly together," Leah said. At first I thought she had just issued me a casual invitation to participate in a threesome. *Who is Molly?* I thought. *Is she your friend with the septum piercing? Is she already on board with this? Do I need to start working out?* Of course, "molly" did not mean Leah's college friend who had moved to Detroit to make house music while living in an unfurnished warehouse and who identified as "sexually omnivorous." In fact, that's not even a person who exists; I had invented her in a panic.

In this case, "molly" referred to the street name for pure MDMA, the active ingredient in ecstasy. You have to hand it to drug dealers: they're always innovating. The problem with ecstasy, apparently, is that while in its pure form it's an intense high and not especially addictive, it's often cut with less expensive drugs like heroin or cocaine. To me, the fact that people used heroin to make a substance *less* potent was terrifying. "Let's get a little of the stuff that killed John Belushi into the mix. Otherwise it might be too much for people," was not a comforting sentiment to me.

"How do we know that there won't be any of that stuff in the molly?" I asked, naively.

"Because then it wouldn't be molly," she explained, shaking her head. It seems like MDMA brings out the sommelier in any peddler of illicit pharmaceuticals. If the grapes aren't from the Champagne region of France, you're not drinking Champagne, and if there's any crushed-up Adderall compounded into your little white tablets, you're not *really* swallowing molly (and don't let your local dealer tell you any different). "It's a nice thing for couples to do," she continued. "They used to use it for therapy. It'll bring us closer together."

Getting closer as a couple sounded appealing, especially since we spent most of our time geographically (and emotionally) remote from one another. The idea of doing drugs, however, was somehow even more stressful to me than the concept of sleeping with two women at once. And yes, I encourage you to take a moment to verify and digest the fact that you have just read the most unfun sentence ever committed to paper. In terms of pure opposition to pleasure and joy, that arrangement of words is right up there with "The amusement park is closing early for routine maintenance!" It is a profoundly square stance to take, one that even Huey Lewis would not defend as hip, and the News would back him up.

At the time, even though I'd started drinking a little, I still had a great deal of self-worth tied up in my identity as a Person Who Does Not Do Drugs. From age seven to twenty-six, I was the friend who knew when to round up the crew and leave the party, the designated driver, the friend who reminded you to drink a glass of water before you went to bed. I spent my youth a paragon of sobriety, my failures and shiftlessness attributable not to any youthful hedonism, but rather to my own natural shortcomings.

It wasn't that I *loved* corralling my drunk friends. It was fear that kept me sober. Fear of what people would say about me. Fear of getting myself into trouble or physical danger. But most of all, it was the fear of losing control. It was less the worry that drugs would lead to a bad time, and more that I'd like them too much. That I'd do something embarrassing or insulting, or that I wouldn't be able to stop once I'd started.

Leading up to my big night out with Leah, I had just a couple of weeks to convince myself it was a good idea to increase my planned New Year's Eve intake of substances from a couple of glasses of wine to a pill powerful enough to prop up the entire genre of electronic dance music. Being me, I went about doing drugs in the nerdiest way possible: thorough and comprehensive research. I started by reading everything I could about MDMA online, which allayed my most visceral fears. And yes, I realize that is about as reliable as pursuing a degree in physics by dropping various household objects off a roof. More important, though, I took an informal survey of my friends, almost all of whom agreed that doing molly one time would not send my life down a slippery slope of addiction and giant red rave pants like it did in every educational film I saw in health class.

The strongest endorsement for MDMA came from my friend Ray. Ray is the kind of guy you call when you have a question you are nervous about asking even Google: "How soon after a one-night stand should I get tested?" "What do you do when you're in the passenger seat and your roommate gets pulled over for drunk driving?" "How do I convince my girlfriend who is on mushrooms that I am not trying to 'interrupt her essence'?" Ray gave me the advice that cemented my decision.

"Joshua, I've done every drug under the sun, and the only one worth doing is ecstasy. I used to do it once a year. I'd call friends I hadn't talked to in a decade and cry and make up. It was the best. I had to stop because the depression the day after was too much. But you're not a sad bastard like me, so drink a lot of water and don't make any plans the next morning."

"Wait, Ray . . . you've done heroin?"

"Once."

"What was *that* like?"

"It was amazing. It was so good I was afraid if I tried it again, I'd just want to do that for the rest of my life, so I never did."

"Wow."

"Yeah, but ecstasy is great. You should try it."

"Okay."

I was convinced. For once in my boring, in-control life, I was going to take a risk, have some fun, live a little, and all the other things your friends say when they're trying to convince you to take a spur-of-the-moment road trip or pay the cover charge at a full-contact strip club with no official address. But I had a good reason. I was going to take illicit, intensely psychoactive drugs, but I was doing it *for love*.

As I write this, I am a grown man. I am married. My life is happy and stable. At the time this happened, though, I was a twenty-five-year-old, which for male humans[1] is like being a tod-

---

1   Not *all* male humans, but . . . plenty of them, the heterosexual ones at least.

dler who can vote and rent cars. I was convinced that my trip to
New York would convey to Leah how cool and spontaneous and
down for whatever I could be in a way that would also make me
seem like a lovable, committed long-term boyfriend. That is a
nonsense goal dreamed up by a child with a debit card. But I was
certain the fate of my relationship was contingent on our New
Year's plans.

The stage was set. We were going to do drugs, like a couple
of rock stars or bored rich teens. Only one problem remained: we
did not have any drugs. I, personally, did not even know where to
get the kind of drugs we were looking for. If it had been as simple
as tracking down some weed, there were semilegitimate delivery
services for that, bike messengers with business cards who would
bring a Whitman's Sampler of marijuana strains right to your door.

But I was skipping straight past the gateway drug of marijuana,
hopping the gate, and tumbling down the slippery slope on the
other side. And while I probably knew someone who knew someone who knew someone who could get their hands on a dose of
MDMA on a day's notice, I was *not* prepared to have the attendant
conversations and deliver the required explanations.

Fortunately, Ben, my girlfriend's ex-boyfriend, was in town
(what a fraught set of feelings!), and we all had dinner plans that
night. He was the Jewish summer camp hippie type, and even
visiting from out of state, he seemed like our best bet for finding a
drug hookup. After an entree's worth of small talk, Leah broached
the question.

"Hey, we were thinking about getting some molly for tomorrow
night. Do you know anyone who might be able to help us out?"

"Hmmm. I have a buddy out in Bushwick who I think has some."

"And it's like, *molly* molly?" Leah pressed.

"Oh yeah, for sure."

Very comforting. A veritable forensic chemical analysis, that was.

So the next day we did what generations of our predecessors had done when they wanted harder drugs than they had immediate access to: we went to Brooklyn. Leah, like many nice Jewish girls who recently graduated from liberal arts institutions, lived with an old friend on the Upper East Side of Manhattan. The apartment was small, with no living room and a bedroom that wrapped around the bed like a suit fits around a body that has gained fifteen pounds since the initial fitting (a metaphor drawn directly from personal experience). The trip out to Bushwick took nearly an hour, and exiting the subway felt like emerging into a different city entirely.

Absent were Manhattan's dense clusters of residential buildings, bagel shops, and bodegas. Bushwick seemed to exist on an entirely warehouse-based economy. Walking through the neighborhood resembled ambling through a particularly grim level of a side-scrolling video game from the 1990s. Row after row of identical, depressing buildings. Even the residences were carved into former industrial behemoths, which had been rezoned to allow people to live in them . . . or, thinking back, maybe they hadn't been. The important thing is, people were living in them.

Nowadays, Bushwick is a hip place where struggling artists can still sometimes afford to live within walking distance of a pour-over coffee shop. But just a few years ago, it was a corner of the city that relatively few transplants had attempted to gentrify.[2] It was a swath of Brooklyn musicians and/or college grads moved to when they didn't have their parents' help paying rent, or at least they didn't want to *look* like they did. It was a place to live until your career in the arts took off, or until the rising tide of "urban renewal" forced you to apply for office jobs.

We pressed the buzzer at the front door of a structure that looked less like an apartment building and more like a haunted steel mill and walked up the stairs to a large, open loft whose decor could best be described as "room where an entire punk band you've never heard of crashes while on tour." Ben's friend greeted us and led us to his corner of the space, which, I must reiterate, had the vibe of an indoor skate park that had recently been condemned.

The three of us sat down and made some awkward small talk, because if you just walk into someone's apartment and request that he sell you drugs, he will think you're a cop. So we had to sit there and listen to this guy—whose name and face I could not, at the time I am writing this, recall at gunpoint—talk about his plans for party-hopping later that night until he deigned to address the entire reason we were sitting in his bedcorner on a sub-Ikea couch:

"So . . . uhhh, Ben said you guys were interested in some molly?"

We nodded, as if to imply, *Yeah, man. Why else would you have answered the door for two strangers?*

---

2   In addition, of course, to the neighborhood's original residents, who have been pushed ever farther to the margins of the borough by those transplants.

"How much do you need?"

I hadn't considered that. A big problem with purchasing controlled substances, it turns out, is that they don't come in standard sizes. You can't ask for a "two pack" or a "youth large" of molly. Buying drugs is like ordering at a tapas restaurant. You need the server to talk you through how much you require depending on your budget, your appetite, and how long you are willing to spend sobbing in the bathroom the next day.

"Enough for two people, but me more than him," Leah explained. "It's his first time." I smiled, slightly embarrassed, the way you feel the last time your mother takes you to a pediatrician before you realize you need a doctor for adults. Whenever I'm about to do something fun, it seems, it's usually my first time.

"Cool. That'll be seventy-five dollars." I handed over the cash, and he gave me a little envelope of white powder, which at the time felt like a bad deal. You can get so much more of so many things for seventy-five dollars. We could have gone out for a lobster dinner. I already knew I would enjoy that. Seventy-five dollars gets you a whole bottle of fancier bourbon than I'd ever tasted before. And a bottle of booze has a satisfying heft to it, not like a tiny little button bag of what looked like decorative sand.

We got back to Leah's apartment with enough time to order a light dinner before we turned around and headed back to Brooklyn for the show. We split some Thai food, changed clothes, and set our sights on our small pouch of contraband.

"So, uhh, how do we . . . you know . . . do it?" I asked.

"I don't know," Leah replied. "I've only ever taken it as pills before."

"Oh."

I felt, not betrayed, but definitely overwhelmed. I thought I was trusting myself in the hands of an expert, but it turned out Leah was more like a pharmacological enthusiast.

"I don't want to snort it," she said.

I hadn't even realized snorting was on the table. That was a high threshold to cross. I was already trying something new. I did not also need to attempt a completely novel way to put things inside me. When it comes to things entering my body, I'm kind of an old-fashioned mouth-only type. Nose isn't even next in the hierarchy of openings through which I would accept recreational substances. That goes: mouth, butt, nose, veins, eyeballs. Putting something in your nose for fun is empirically gross, whether it's your own finger, a psychoactive powder, or a Cheerio (oh, like you never did that when you were three years old).

"I guess we could Google what to do?" I offered, like a real dork. So we did, once again turning the prospect of an evening of carefree debauchery into a research paper. Google, as is its custom, provided a plethora of results that ranged from helpful to total nonsense. Snorting the powder, as we suspected, was bad news, as was rubbing it on your gums in the way a police officer in a movie checks to see if cocaine is really cocaine. Apparently that can erode your gums and damage the enamel on your teeth. Be more careful, movie cops!

The method that seemed safest and least reminiscent of *Trainspotting* was what the internet called "parachuting," which, despite what you may imagine, is not a fetish that involves having sex with your old gym teacher while wrapped in one of those rainbow parachutes. It instead constitutes tearing off a square inch of toilet paper, wrapping the drugs inside it, and then dropping the little package down your throat, like you're sending aid into a war zone. I will say again, swallowing a square of toilet paper was the *least* gross and *most* appealing option.

We decided to gulp down half the powder before we left and save half to take in the bathroom at the venue if the first dose wore off. We tore a square of Leah's postcollege one-ply toilet paper into little parcels, divided out two tiny piles of white powder, hers a little bigger than mine, and threw them back. We tucked the rest of our stash (a very small amount by this point) into Leah's purse and set off into the night.

There I found myself, on the streets of New York City, doing drugs like a Sex Pistol or one of the gangsters from *American Gangster*, which I haven't seen but hear good things about and should really put in my Netflix queue. I was finally seizing the night, like Smirnoff Ice ads had been encouraging me to do for years.

Now, when someone who likes fun finds himself in those circumstances, I imagine his internal monologue goes something like this: "WOOOOOOOOOOOOOOOO!"

My antsy, controlling brain, however, sounded more like this: "Okay. I'm on drugs. So far so good. I mean, it's no better or worse than normal. I think? How long do drugs take to kick in? Did I take enough drugs for them to work? Did I throw a half day's worth of preschool salary down the drain? That thought makes me queasy. Or are the *drugs* making me queasy? Are they working? Is this what drugs are like? I don't think I like drugs. Or maybe this is just the first part. Maybe this is the ecstasy overture. The overture is never the best part. I bet it gets better. But what if it's all overture?" Oh, that was also my external monologue. That train ride was a real treat for Leah, I'm sure.

We arrived at the venue, which was a large bowling alley with a stage at the far end where the band would perform. There was a little café where concertgoers could buy pizza and beer. The whole scene was very "2010s Brooklyn" in that it was something that could be found in any major city in America, but here it was slightly fancier and vastly more expensive. We each got a cup of water from the bar because that's what you are supposed to drink when you are on drugs, even if the drugs you are on haven't started to feel like drugs yet.

"Should we be feeling it by now?" I asked.

"I think it's about to kick in. I'm getting that feeling that you get before you start feeling it for real. It's kind of warm. Do you feel warm?"

"I think so, but I'm still wearing my coat."

"Well, do you want to do more? I think I'm going to do some more."

So we took turns ducking into the unisex bathroom to swaddle a little more powder in toilet paper and gulp it down, which by this point had started to feel like a trick someone would play if they were trying to get you to eat a roll of toilet paper. We reconvened on the dance floor.

"Still nothing?"

"Nothing. You?"

"Nothing."

Several minutes past the advertised showtime, the stage remained dark. We stood toward the back of the thickening crowd, quietly willing the chemicals we'd ingested to enter our bloodstreams . . . or release dopamine from our brains . . . into our brains? Even now, I'm not exactly sure how drugs work, which makes me feel shaky about my decision to have taken them.

Finally, nearly an hour after the show was scheduled to start, the Roots took the stage. You may know the Roots primarily from their current gig as megafamous laughers at Jimmy Fallon's monologue jokes, but the reason they are on television every night is because they are the best band. They are a hip-hop group, but one that can, at the snap of a snare drum, lock into any groove that has ever been written. It has been said that writing about music is like dancing about architecture, but sometimes you see a building that makes you think, *I need to physically express my awe at this structure through dance*, and in that spirit, here is my attempt to capture the experience of seeing the Roots live.

Black Thought, the group's front man, possesses two singular gifts as a rapper. Number one: he can make any two words rhyme. It's amazing. In the song "Adrenaline" he pairs "auction" with "chicken szechuan" and the effect isn't (as you might expect) "Dude, those words don't really rhyme. You've got to try that again." It is instead "How did I never notice that those two words rhyme perfectly?" Gift number two: he does not need to breathe. He raps with the same ceaseless and tireless energy that the Colorado River used to gouge the Grand Canyon into the sandstone of the Arizona desert. The group's most famous member is, of course, ?uestlove, notable for his voluminous Afro, his work recording music with everyone from Lin-Manuel Miranda to D'Angelo, and for giving off the impression that he could smash out a backbeat on a drum kit consisting of a broken DVD player, a memory foam pillow, and a taxidermied rabbit. Between Thought's vocals and ?uest's percussion there's a full ensemble (keys, bass, guitar, and more) that plays with the momentum of a bowling ball thundering down a spiral staircase. When you hear it, you don't get in the way; you fucking *move*.

Leah and I moved. I do not dance often. I am so self-conscious about how bad I am at it that I can rarely get my body parts working in sync with one another. I think, *I should move my hips*, and there they go, but then I focus so hard on that I forget about my upper body. *Oh shit, wiggle your shoulders, you weirdo*, my brain commands, and once I start, the rest of me goes rigid. It feels like some kind of mindfulness meditation exercise and looks like a mannequin coming slowly to life, limb by limb.

On December 31, 2010, however, I danced with my whole body at once. To onlookers I imagine it seemed as if Leah were made of electricity, and any point of contact with her sent a powerful shock through me. The relentless beat caused unexpected quakes and tremors in my body, as if endorphins were being physically fracked out of me. As I joyfully approximated dancing for the next hour, I began to wonder: Was I on drugs after all?

When the band finished their first set and left the stage, my mood returned to its normal level, which I can best describe as "happy, but would be happier if I were eating pizza." So Leah and I ordered pizza from the bowling alley/concert venue's café, a sentence that forever settles any debates about whether I am a millennial. I enjoyed the pizza slightly more than I usually do, but I attributed it to the addition of pulled pork as a topping rather than any chemical enhancement.

Then, when the Roots took the stage again, I hurried back to the dance floor. *That* was a little weird. To me, a dance floor is like a Subway sandwich shop: I will spend time there only if I have no other options. At weddings, even the most crowd-pleasing song (which is "I Wanna Dance with Somebody [Who Loves Me]" by Whitney Houston) can barely drag me out of my seat. The Roots played three sets, and each time they appeared onstage, my heart rate rose and I was swept up in a riptide of enthusiasm. Then, when the music stopped, the euphoria began to ebb. After the band's second set, I made an embarrassing realization. My new experience for the night wasn't "doing drugs" after all. But I had managed to dabble in "having a good time."

By midnight, Leah and I had become fairly convinced that we hadn't taken any of the kind of powerful psychoactive substances that necessitated constant hydration and prohibited drinking alcohol. I felt pretty confident about this because my mental state was such that I was still concerned with proper hydration as opposed to which people, objects, or ideas I could rub up against for maximum physical pleasure.

Relatively certain we weren't in any imminent danger, Leah and I decided to participate in the champagne toast when the clock struck midnight. We clinked glasses of whatever vintage is handed out at bowling alleys in Brooklyn, as the Roots emerged to play "Auld Lang Syne," "When the Saints Go Marching In," and several other standards, backed by a full-on brass ensemble.

The single glass of champagne sent me almost immediately from zero to "Hooray!" where I settled comfortably for the rest of the night.

The last note of the final encore receded into the night around three o'clock, at which point ?uestlove announced that after a short break, he would reemerge and deejay until 7:30 a.m. Even by the most generous allowances, that is significantly past my bedtime. By my estimation, once a party approaches the length of a full day in an office, any amount of Having Fun is still essentially Doing Work. Leah and I agreed that staying out until three in the morning after trying to do drugs constituted a successful New Year's Eve, and it was time to head home.

We walked out into 2011 for the first time. It was cold and dark, as most years are at the beginning. It also felt hopeful and full of potential. In exactly seven months, I would live in New York City, a big step that started to feel more possible after New Year's Eve. I felt capable of anything that night, except for catching a cab back to Manhattan.

We were still living in (as unimaginable as it sounds) a pre-Uber world, so the process of finding someone to drive you home consisted of the draconian method of shooting your hand into the sky like a fleshy road flare. Finally, at four a.m., we arrived back at Leah's apartment. As final proof we were not on ecstasy, we fell asleep without having sex.

The next morning, Leah texted Ben that his friend had sold us bogus molly. Hours later, when he woke up, he replied:

Bummer. You got a blank postcard.

At first that felt like kind of a cute stoner euphemism for his friend screwing us out of seventy-five dollars. But with time, "blank postcard" has made more and more sense to me. What we'd paid for wasn't the uniform tourist experience of taking MDMA. Instead we'd spent seventy-five bucks for the chance to fill in the space as we saw fit, and we managed to make it uniquely special and lovely.

Still, that New Year's Eve provided a microcosm of why Leah and I eventually broke up. My ceiling for excitement was her floor. We were always slightly off, two words listed as synonyms under the same thesaurus entry that weren't quite interchangeable. I was trying to be a partner; she wanted an accomplice. She was out for an experience; I turned it into an experiment. I was Doing Drugs; she was just going out.[3] Those two things are technically the same, but they also very much are not. Exactly what I thought would make me Boyfriend Material is what made me a bad boyfriend in this situation.

It's hard to want different things from someone you're dating, but it's somehow also hard to want the same thing but for different reasons. That's something I learned in a unisex bathroom at a bowling alley-slash-music venue as I swallowed a square inch of toilet paper wrapped around Ajax or crushed up Advil or rat poison or whatever it was I actually ingested. In the long run, trying to do a drug to bring us closer highlighted the chasm between us, and no matter how much fun we had that night, it wouldn't cause enough of a tectonic shift to close that gap.

---

3 No one expressed this type of dichotomy better than 50 Cent when he rapped, "I'm into having sex / I ain't into making love."

Years later, I hope the guy who sold us the fake molly is still living in a semihabitable warehouse in Bushwick. Yes, I mean that mostly as a hipster curse, but I also think the world needs him there, dispensing psychedelics and placebos depending on what he perceives the needs of the customer to be, teaching them something about themselves in the process.

But it's been eight years, so by now it's more likely his band has broken up and he works for a hedge fund.

Things I Have Tried (with Varying Degrees of Success) at the Behest of Women I Was Dating at the Time or to Whom I Am Married

Dancing
MDMA
Oysters
Moulin Rouge!
Riding a bike for the first time in ten years
   (not as easy as popular wisdom suggests)
Getting a massage
Sushi
Enjoying the beach
Being slapped in the face during sexual intercourse
   (I did not try this by choice.)
Having a dog
A Disney cruise
Celebrating Christmas
Going to the gym
Seeing other people for a little while
Paying a little extra for the direct flight

Good Will Hunting Isn't Science Fiction

It was ten o'clock on December 31, 2014, and I had taken the stage in front of a sold-out crowd of 1,100ish at the Wilbur Theater on Tremont Street in Boston's theater district. The audience was not there to see me. They were there to see John Oliver, a much more famous and successful comedian, who was also my boss at the time. But—*surprise!*—they had to sit through fifteen minutes of me first. I wore a suit because these people had come for a "night out on the town." I had drunk one glass of whiskey, because I was *also* out on the town.

"Thank you," I began, as the unearned round of applause that begins most shows died down. "It's so lovely to be here with you tonight. I grew up just outside the city, and I started stand-up here, so it's really meaningful to me to get to be here in this beautiful theater with you tonight, on New Year's Eve."

The crowd applauded again. I would contend that I didn't earn that ovation, either. Anybody can pander to the hometown crowd.

"That said," I continued, "I did move to New York about three years ago because I wanted to be happy and successful."

The audience booed, which I will admit I deserved. I smiled, waiting for the jeers to crest and begin diminishing.

"Oh, come on," I twisted the knife, "you don't get to boo me. Anyone is allowed to leave. *Good Will Hunting* isn't science fiction." I wasn't wrong. You can leave your hometown if you're not satisfied with your life there. Just ask every Bruce Springsteen song.

Despite my being objectively correct, the audience's disapproval rained down on me again. I luxuriated in their contempt. I'd achieved what professional wrestling fans call "heel heat," a visceral engagement with the audience based on their excitement to hate you. I'd never had that before.

In three and a half years, New York had made me a worse person, and I was all the better for it.

Sorry, Not Sorry

On New Year's Eve 2014, a little more than three years after moving to New York, I made a single, unambiguous resolution: I decided to stop apologizing when people bumped into me. It sounds like a simple rule to follow, but it proved deceptively hard to abide by. I am an apologetic person by nature. I apologize to inanimate objects I collide with. I apologize for taking up people's time in emails they have specifically asked me to send them. I apologize to my dog for not being able to give her more treats, no matter how insistently she sneezes in my face.

I'm not especially religious, but my favorite part of Judaism is the time between Rosh Hashanah and Yom Kippur, when you're expected to make amends for any slights you've committed over the previous year. A week of scheduled, regimented apology. My dream. I used to fulfill this obligation with a mass email to friends and family members, expressing contrition and asking forgiveness. One time, I accidentally sent it without bcc-ing the recipients, so everyone could see who was on the list. I sent a follow-up email apologizing for that.

The change came slowly, but it did come. A few months after my "no apologies" declaration, I was transferring subway lines at the Times Square station, which is a little like squeezing through the bar at the *Star Wars* cantina, but with worse music, and you're directly underneath a Bubba Gump Shrimp Co. I joined the human colloid spilling out of the downtown A train. As I stepped onto the platform, another passenger bumped me shoulder to shoulder as he squeezed onto the train, not hard, but hard enough.

Now, if you do not live in a place with abundant public transportation, here's the problem with that: the rule is, you let everyone off the train, and then you get on the train. There are no exceptions to this rule. I realize that we live in a highly individualized society, where we are alienated from communities and encouraged to look out primarily for ourselves. But without accepted norms, we do not have a society at all; we are living in anarchy.

If you push through the torrent of disembarking passengers to get aboard a subway train fifteen seconds sooner, you are a true sociopath. You're the kind of person who would drive on the left side of the highway because there's less traffic going that way, or who would wear another person's actual human face as a Halloween costume.

So, one of those kinds of people jostled me as he psychopathed his way onto the train, probably on his way to dump a barrel of crude oil into a lake just to see the swirling colors. My body contorting from the glancing contact, I swiveled my head to face the reckless commuter.

"Sorry!" I called after him.

But the thing is: I *wasn't* sorry. In fact, it was *he* who should have apologized to *me*. Something inside me broke, like a dog's leash snapping in two, allowing for unfettered pursuit of a mail carrier or a squirrel or some other formidable dog nemesis.

"HEY!" I shouted into the train, as the *bing-bong* chime sounded and the doors began to close. "I'M NOT ACTUALLY SORRY!" Adrenaline flooded my body. I felt powerful, limitless, a subway etiquette vigilante, standing up for himself and for all New Yorkers.

Over the next couple of years, I did not become a renegade passenger, enforcing the mores of the underground with gentle rebukes from behind closed doors. I did, however, manage to curtail my compulsive and unnecessary apologies. I also got more conscientious about finding old people to whom I could offer my seat and then shooting *very judgy looks* at the people who didn't, but that's beside the point.

On Halloween night 2016, I felt for the first time like a Real New Yorker. Granted, the "Real New Yorker" is kind of a mythical concept. Some would argue that unless you were born there, you'll never be one. Others claim you can earn your Real New Yorker stripes if you've done enough Real New York City Shit. For example, fistfighting Joey Ramone over a slice of pizza or peeing on the street next to Lou Reed, who then winks and tosses a bag of heroin neatly into your shirt pocket.

The city is changing, with shifting demographics and rising income inequality. In a lot of ways, the culture and grit has been scrubbed away from it. Opportunities are evaporating for all but

the richest and most privileged, which is alarming. But longtime
New York residents often romanticize things that don't even seem
good. "You used to be able to get your dick sucked for a nickel in
any building south of Forty-Fifth Street," they might lament, "but
now some of those places are ATMs."

Or: "Back in my day, just to get on the crosstown bus, you had
to let an NYPD officer punch your mother in the face and then
tip your hat to him. God, I miss Giuliani."

My Real New York moment came unexpectedly, which I think
they always do. I had taken the L train from Brooklyn into Manhattan. The L runs from the West Side of Manhattan through
north Brooklyn and out to Canarsie. Along its stops from west to
east in Brooklyn, clusters of cafés serving vegan baked goods have
spread like blood poisoning down a vein.[1] Rents along the subway line have risen, contributing to the difficulty of living in the
city. And I'm sure there's also a contingent that's purely nostalgic
for the days before Brooklyn's Bushwick neighborhood was dotted
with tattoo parlors and yoga studios, when you could simply walk
up and down the unlit streets and get murdered in any abandoned
warehouse you wanted.

I hopped off the train at Sixth Avenue, and instead of transferring to go one stop south, I climbed the stairs to street level, eager
to clear my head on the eleven-block walk through the warm October night. Unfortunately, I found myself on the wrong side of a
parade. That's not a figure of speech. Being surprised by parades
is a not insignificant part of living in New York. Normally, you feel

---

1   I'm not against vegan baked goods, just their customary price point.

like an asshole for getting mad at them because they're celebrating things like LGBTQ pride or Puerto Rican heritage. When you get mad at the traffic caused by those parades, you're basically being racist and homophobic.

A Halloween parade, however, is just a nuisance. What kid even wants to be part of a parade on Halloween night? It just means you still have to go through the effort of getting into costume without the benefit of your neighbors giving you candy on demand. I should have ducked back into the train station and emerged from the exit on the opposite side of Sixth Avenue. Instead, I started walking south, totally confident that at some point someone would let me cross the goddamn Halloween parade, an entity whose integrity could not possibly mean anything to anyone.

As I walked, the crowd of spectators grew thicker. Thousands of people had shown up to watch costumed revelers march by, which felt ridiculous to me because it was Halloween, so they could have seen that *anywhere*. City workers had set up metal barriers along the route to protect the integrity of a phalanx of seven-year-olds dressed as the grim reaper. Every few blocks, I encountered a police checkpoint where an officer assured me that at the *next* checkpoint I'd be allowed to cross. I'd already wriggled twenty blocks downtown when it dawned on me that I'd probably have to go all the way around the parade, which would entail making my way to Canal Street, almost a mile and a half from where I started.

I'd left myself plenty of time to make the trip from my apartment in Williamsburg to Greenwich Village under normal circumstances, but with the distance the parade had added to the trip, I was running late. I slogged west to Seventh Avenue, where the sidewalks didn't so much resemble clogged arteries, and I broke into a jog.

After a few minutes I had become moderately winded and more-than-moderately sweaty, but I was making decent time, weaving between trick-or-treating kids and drunk-in-costume adults, when I came across a Halloween Asshole. A Halloween Asshole is the kind of person who wants the credit of dressing up without actually wearing a costume. You see them every year. Frat guys in dresses. Women with kitty cat ears. Anyone in a rainbow Afro wig. Everyone is on to you, Halloween Assholes. And no one is impressed.

This particular Halloween Asshole was wearing a Bernie Sanders 2016 campaign T-shirt,[2] and in each hand he held a strand of Mardi Gras beads, which he twirled like nunchucks. I couldn't even figure out what he was going for, cumulatively. Was it some kind of visual pun? Was he a Socialist Party Animal? Did New Orleans plus Vermont add up to the Big Cheesy? Although, we were in New York City—maybe he didn't even know it was Halloween, and that's just how he dressed in his everyday life. Maybe he was just a Regular Asshole.

Regardless of this guy's confusing outfit, I had to get around him. I jogged past, giving him what would have been a plenty wide berth, had he not been spinning Mardi Gras beads around like a dipshit. Unfortunately, he was indeed spinning Mardi Gras beads around like a dipshit, and one of the strands of studded translucent

---

2   Remember: this was one week before the 2016 presidential election, and Bernie Sanders had ended his campaign several months earlier.

plastic whipped me in the neck. It didn't leave a mark, but it did infringe on the cardinal rule of New York City sidewalks: "Stay out of my way, dickhead."

"Sorry," he said, but not like you say it when you're sorry. He spit out the word as if it meant "Uhhh . . . I'm inventing a new martial art here . . . idiot."

After half a decade as a New York resident, I was intimately familiar with the word "sorry" as an act of aggression, a middle finger disguised as a thumbs-up.

"There's train traffic ahead of us. Sorry for the delay. We hope to be moving shortly."

"Sorry to bail last minute after you definitely already left the house to meet me at the place *I* suggested for drinks that's nowhere near your apartment. A work thing came up. Let's reschedule for soon!"

"Sorry, we don't have 'iced coffee,' just cold brew." Come on. Cold brew is just coffee with ice in it. Just give me your pretentious, overpriced iced coffee, and spare me your condescension, please.

I don't know what it was about this particular indignity that made me so furious. Maybe it was the self-indulgent nature of the way he was hogging the sidewalk. Maybe it was the fact that I had planned so carefully and yet still found myself behind schedule, and this guy was slowing me down further. Maybe it was the fact that my chest had started pounding after a quarter-mile jog and sweat had rendered my back as slick and damp as the cheese on a Greek pizza, and I was really just disappointed in myself. Maybe it was the sheer laziness of his Halloween costume. But something about this guy brought out a level of rage I'd never expressed to a stranger before.

What I wish I'd yelled was, "Hey, you're a socialist, right? Well then, redistribute the sidewalk, asshole!"

What I actually yelled was much less clever: "Hey, man! Fuck you!"

The words surprised me as they came out of my mouth. Bernie Gras 2016 was not surprised. I imagine it's because he seemed like the kind of guy people yelled "Fuck you!" at a lot.

"I said sorry!" he shouted back, as if he'd done something totally reasonable, like accidentally bumping into my table at a coffee shop, or stepping on my sneaker on a crowded train car. He had not done something reasonable. He had hit me in the neck with Mardi Gras beads, which, by the way, are *the paraphernalia of a totally different holiday*. When you are the one who's being a jerk, you have to both apologize *and* allow the person you have wronged to curse you out. Those are the rules.

"Yeah, and *then* I said 'Fuck you!'" I yelled, just to clarify the timeline. It wasn't that I'd missed his apology. I had heard it and rejected it.

I was uninterested in whether he wanted to offer another response. I didn't want to *fight* this guy, and our conversation seemed to have reached a stalemate. I was proud of myself as I ran, like I'd finally gotten comfortable enough to lay into someone who legitimately deserved it in true New York fashion. In his retelling of the story, I am probably the asshole, which is another typical New York City feeling: the other guy is always the asshole.

But that *still* didn't make me a local. After all, people curse

each other out on the street all over the world. The feeling of belonging came two years later.

I was walking across the street (at a crosswalk, with the light
on my side, despite my Boston-bred love of jaywalking), when a
woman quickly gunned her engine to muscle past me in an expensive SUV. Reflexively, I flipped out my middle finger and held it
up to her driver's side window until she'd passed me. I felt nothing.
I was at peace. In that instant, I was a Real New Yorker.

Gap Years

When my sister, Jenna, was born, I was just about three weeks from my third birthday. For twenty-four hours, I was 1,078 times older than she was. Mathematically speaking, it was the most older-than-her I have ever been. Practically, though, there was not a *ton* of meaningful difference between our ages. Yes, I had become a proficient walker and talker as I approached my third birthday. And not to toot my own horn, but I'd gotten pretty decent at eating solid foods. But I couldn't read or tie my shoes, and I stood barely tall enough to operate the average doorknob. So any edge in maturity that my head start in the world gave me was slim at best.

Over the course of our lives, those three years dilated and contracted, sometimes feeling like a decade, other times like an instant. On occasion, time seemed to reverse its flow entirely.

In any functional sense, the age gap between Jenna and me was most pronounced while we were both in high school. Even though our age difference has technically always been almost exactly three years, Jenna was fussy and brainy enough as a toddler that she skipped a year of preschool, and from that point on we were only two grades apart. By my senior year, the two of us had such full calendars of extracurricular activities that our schedules functioned only if I took over a little of the responsibility that had previously fallen on my parents.

Some of the outsourcing was informational. My mom and dad, to an extent, considered me their eyes and ears on the ground that was our social landscape. So if Jenna asked permission to go to a party, they would consult me, their honest and boring son, regarding whether the gathering was appropriate for their daughter. She, being not much more fun or exciting than I was, rarely tried to con her way into attending any event that was too rowdy or unsavory, so the answer was almost always "Sure."

My chief task as an older sibling, though, was to transport Jenna to and from dance class. Two or three times a week, we'd rush from our last classes to the high school parking lot and then race to the little dance studio in the next town over. "Race," I admit, is a strong word for the way I drove. I was a timid pilot of my dad's 1986 Honda Accord (the kind with the headlights that blink open and close like a robot face), and I never exceeded the speed limit. In fact, often, just to be safe, I drove three to five miles per hour below the legally allowed speed. Other drivers commended my safety by beeping their horns in solidarity and waving to me with one finger (so as not to obscure their vision of the road with a full open hand, I imagine). Usually I'd then have to putter back to school, rehearse for a play or attend a yearbook meeting or pretend to be sad to miss a math team practice.

Because of our frequent trips in the car and the length to which my deliberately paced driving prolonged them, we had plenty of time to complain about our coursework and gossip about

Jenna's friends. And, in the grand tradition of older brothers, I forced her to listen to the music I liked. It wasn't the *classic* older brother stuff. (I never took a rip from a bong and said, "Fuckin' Zeppelin, man. Get ready to shit your brain out your ears.") But I certainly imposed on her with plenty of Weezer and Ben Folds Five (a Stoneham High School drama club mainstay). She operated the Discman connected to the car's speakers through an adapter shaped like a cassette, the way Rube Goldberg might play music in whatever fanciful, impractical car he drove. We stumbled through wordy verses and belted out choruses together as I drove, hands dutifully at ten and two, knuckles white from the effort of gripping the steering wheel. From school to the dance studio, then later from the dance studio back home for dinner.

Our family, whenever possible, ate dinner together until I left for college, which felt very *Wonder Years*, even at the time. I almost wanted to ask my parents: "What's your deal? Are we doing this because you saw it on TV?" Presence was never *demanded* of me and my sister, but it was *expected* if at all possible. I don't know what there was to talk about five nights a week with people you saw every day, but I do know that I did most of the talking. A family dinner with me was like the experience of listening to the audio version of this book, plus spaghetti.

I didn't realize quite the extent of my dominance over the dinner table conversation until I'd gone away to college. Soon after I'd left for Brandeis, Jenna, the more reserved of the two Gondelman siblings, and I were talking on the phone.

"Mom and dad have a *lot* more questions for me at dinner now that you're not around," she said.

"You mean like they trust you less?"

"No, it's just like . . . there's a lot more silence to fill."

Jenna enrolled at Brandeis two years later. The gap between our ages both stayed the same and began to close. The difference between a college freshman and a college junior is so much smaller than the difference between a high school freshman and a high school junior. Mostly it's that the junior can legally buy alcohol and has started to feel the creeping dread of the real world beginning to take hold.

"Isn't it weird to go to college with your little sister?" friends would ask. And honestly, it wasn't. We had very few overlapping academic interests; she took mostly science classes, while I avoided any course that involved numbers (besides the ones that tell you what page you're on). So it wasn't like our professors were comparing us. And, just as in high school, neither of us really drank, so the chances of one of us stumbling across the other doing something embarrassing on campus were slim, with the exception of her choosing to attend my improv shows. She and her friends often came to my shows on campus, and I proudly went to see her perform with the school's tap-dancing ensemble, HOT (Hooked On Tap). Mercifully for both of us, neither she nor I decided to pursue a cappella.

There were a few awkward moments. My childhood best friend and freshman-year roommate, Ethan, nearly passed out when Jenna showed up at a keg party in his dorm our junior year. (*Jenna Gondelman*, he gasped. *No no no no no.*) But mostly things were very nice.

Then, in a brief reversal after college during my late twenties, my little sister became (effectively) older than I was. When Jenna received her doctorate at age twenty-four, I was twenty-seven and had been living in New York City for almost a year. New York, if you're unfamiliar, is the urban equivalent of a tapeworm for your bank account and self-esteem.[1] While my sister finished grad school and parlayed an internship into a full-time position at a major hospital, my income came in dribbles through my various gigs tutoring, doing stand-up, and freelance magazine writing. And while cash trickled into my bank account, my savings hemorrhaged back out the way beer gushes from a can that's been stabbed with the key at a frat party.

It wasn't just my bank balance that was moving in the wrong direction. My stand-up career, which had crept steadily forward while I lived in Boston, had taken a step backward as well. Though I had some paid work on the road, I spent most nights in New York shuttling from open mic to open mic, performing for half-full rooms of other comedians, many of whom half paid attention to the same jokes from the same people several times a night in different venues across the city. Every night played out like the first half of *Groundhog Day*, after the despair set in but before Bill Murray became suicidal.

I'd also been dumped just a few months after my move, and I was a lot lonelier than I realized. My roommates were night owls who always stayed up until one or two in the morning. Several nights a week I'd fall asleep in the living room while they watched movies or old WWF pay-per-view matches. I often woke up to the

---

1   Technically there are also museums and plays and parks and stuff.

sound of the TV turning off for the night, and I got up and put myself to bed in my actual bed. At the time, I assumed I was just too exhausted to get up and brush my teeth once I'd staked out a spot on the couch. Only years later did it dawn on me that I was doing that because I wanted to be near other people as long as I could.

Throughout that period, Jenna helped keep me on track. Mom and dad's anniversary is next week, she'd text me. Did you get them anything? Should I put your name on my card? Or, Are you coming home for Aunt Barbara's Hanukkah party this year? She needs a head count.

To return the favor, I'd gift her albums over iTunes whenever I stumbled across an artist I thought she might like. It was a small way I could still big brother her from afar.

Those years were like grad school for me, too. Except instead of tuition, I spent my money on rent and bodega cold cut sandwiches and Dunkin' Donuts iced coffees. And instead of a degree I got . . . You know what? It wasn't that much like grad school. But the work over my first few years in New York did (eventually) pay off. I now have a steady job writing comedy for television. I perform at many of the city's fine comedy clubs, often earning dozens of dollars in a single night. I rarely fall asleep on the couch anymore; I sleep in bed with my wife, Maris, and our dog, Bizzy, who weighs only twenty-four pounds and whose only trick is dominating 50 percent of a queen-size mattress.

Now Jenna and I are basically the same age again. Once you hit twenty-five, three years isn't a meaningful difference anymore unless you're on opposite sides of a legal presidential run or the ability to collect social security benefits. We both have full-time jobs and do our own laundry. We often split the cost of birthday and anniversary presents for our parents down the middle. I have a dog, but Jenna owns her apartment, which feels like a stalemate on the adulthood front.

Early last year, I decided to make a quick visit to Massachusetts to see my parents. Jenna picked me up at the Back Bay train station downtown. I hopped into the passenger seat of her car, and she began to navigate the city's ludicrous tangle of one-way streets with calm expertise. (We were just a few blocks from the impossibly Bostonian intersection of Tremont Street and Tremont Street, a traffic pattern seemingly designed to inspire existential despair.) We moved through the city in short bursts, the way you work a blob of toothpaste out of a nearly empty tube, and Jenna remained calm as she drove and we caught up. *I've been gone a long time*, I thought.

But my big brother instincts quickly kicked in.

"Do you mind?" I asked, but without waiting I dug out the aux cord from her car's center console and began to pick the music.

Third Time's
a Charm?

The Three True Stories of How We Met

I can't recommend this strategy to everyone, but once I resolved to start drinking more, my life improved right away.

My specific resolution was to embrace new experiences and make more of a point to accept friends' invitations to fun social events. But people kept inviting me to bars on weeknights, so saying yes to life took the form of a lot of well whiskey (short for "well . . . it's technically whiskey") on the rocks, chased the next morning with vats of Dunkin' Donuts iced coffee clutched tight in my gloved hand (and after the alcohol but before the caffeine, I slept on a bed with no sheets, just a mattress pad and a comforter). It was already March, but winter in New York City lasts as long as it wants. And I, equally stubborn, refuse to not drink cold beverages, even when it's untenable to hold them in my bare hands. I was a frigid mess, which is like a hot mess, but cold.

At the same time, I pretty much stopped cleaning my room, which is also not usually a decision that comes concurrent with major life improvements. After almost three years of cohabitation with three friends in a large but poorly maintained apartment, I decided that by my thirtieth birthday, I'd find a place of my own. And the best way to make sure I followed through was to make my personal space progressively less livable, until I couldn't bear it any longer and had to move. And as a recently single serial monogamist, I hoped that lowering my standard of living would cause me too much shame to invite anyone back to my place. I'd stay unattached and focus on my career and relearn how to live like a human being in my future home.

Two months earlier, adopting a libertine lifestyle wouldn't have been a problem. I had nowhere to be in the morning, since I was making a living (a generous description of my level of income, by the way) freelance writing, tutoring in the afternoon, and doing stand-up on the road. So I could have slept in to my heart's content, or at the very least until the sunlight poked me in the eye through my borderline-translucent blinds.

But then I got hired at the first full-time day job I'd had in three years (the impetus for my decision/ability to move out of my apartment), which meant that I had to be at a place, on time, five days a week. It was, in my opinion, a bit much.

On the other hand, though, the job did provide me with enough money to have as many undergraduate-quality cocktails as I wanted (usually between zero and two) and the occasional taxi home, a *major* step up from the NYC subway, which, after eleven p.m. arrives on time as often as a divorced dad who can't keep track of when it's his week to pick you up from soccer practice. So, on balance, full-time employment was a *slight* negative in terms of the quantity of fun I was able to have in the last year of my twenties, but a huge positive in terms of the quality of that fun.

Anyway, that's why, depending on who's asking, there are the three different versions of how I met my wife.

The Short-and-Sweet Version

First there's the story we tell to strangers and distant relatives. It's quick and to the point. The details are well rehearsed, and there's no messiness. It goes like this:

Drew, a mutual friend, invited me to a party that my now-wife was throwing. She (Drew, a lady, which I should have mentioned before) *couldn't believe* that Maris and I didn't already know each other. I was on my way from a stand-up show in Brooklyn back to my apartment in Harlem, and the party was almost on my route, which made it a perfect "embrace new experiences" quasi-adventure. Because I arrived on the later end of the evening, I was able to have a long conversation with the hostess, and we got along immediately.

I mentioned how earlier that day I'd booked a gig in Sweden, which I was excited about because I'd never been to Europe before.

"I want to go to Sweden!" said Maris, to whom I am now married.

"Okay, so come with me," I said, with a casual confidence that I'd never previously displayed for a moment in my sweaty, anxious life. I added, "But then, why don't you give me your phone number? That way we can hang out once before that in America and make sure we don't hate each other."

That was, without a doubt, the coolest thing I'd ever said, and maybe the only time I've been cool at all. Maris did not join me in Sweden, which is just as well; my entire immediate family came

along, which would have made for an awkward first date. But I did
text her the day after the party. We got brunch two days after that,
and we've been together ever since.

What a nice story, right? It's got everything you want from a
first meeting with a soul mate: a setup by a mutual friend, instant
chemistry, charming banter. What more could you want?

Well, for starters, I guess there's . . . the rest of the story.

The Computer-Literate Version

When younger, more internet-savvy friends and acquaintances ask
how Maris and I met, we usually start with a more complete version of the truth, which is that we knew each other from Twitter.
That's a sentence that's hard to type, and nearly impossible to say
out loud. It's slightly embarrassing, and also hard to explain. It's
like telling people you met at a cockfight or by bumping into each
other reaching for the same pair of orthopedic shoes.

Twitter, if you don't know, is a social media platform on which
users post and share short bursts of text (280 characters, but back
in my day it was only 140) along with embedded photos and video.
It's where I've learned about some of my favorite writers (Doreen
St. Félix! Shea Serrano!) and met some of the people who went on
to be my real-life friends (Jazmine Hughes! Ian Karmel!). On the
other hand, it's also an abyss from the depths of which the world's
worst people howl racist and sexist (and all other manner of) ob-
scenities at total strangers.

In addition to giving a microphone to a faction of the populace
with the intellectual clout and moral compass of Donald Trump's

nutsack (a reason why, if Twitter's headquarters sank into a hole in the ground and its servers exploded like Fourth of July fireworks while its employees escaped safely from the rubble, I would not be upset), Twitter also functions as a pretty decent dating app. It's effective, mostly, because it's not trying to be a dating app. You interact with strangers, but you don't see the Tinder version[1] of them.

On an intentional dating app, people put what they consider their best, most fuckable foot forward (this is not literally about foot fucking; I assume there's a different app for that). That can mean anything from posing next to a fancy car, to listing your height, to exclusively having pictures with more attractive friends, as if to say, "Good-looking people want to be close to me. Are you in, or are you ugly?" On Twitter, people feel more empowered to be their horrible selves. Or, at least, they do it all the time by accident. You get to see their worst opinions on politics, art, airline delays, and themselves. People tweet their random bizarre thoughts when they're bored. They post their pettiest complaints when they're inconvenienced. You get a much more thorough view of people than just learning that they "love to travel."

So, before I ever met Maris, I knew of her from Twitter, which means I knew she was well read and sarcastic (but not "fluent in sarcasm," as assholes claim to be in their online bios) and pretty and enthusiastic and feminist.[2] I knew of her blog, *Slaughterhouse*

---

1   Or the FarmersOnly.com version, if that's more your speed.
2   Obviously she has more fine qualities, too! She is also supportive and independent and generous and thoughtful and silly and insightful and good at dancing and great at karaoke, but I didn't know any of that at the time.

90210, a sharp and charming mashup of images from television and quotes from literature. The party we met at was in honor of *Slaughterhouse*'s fifth anniversary. She, most likely, knew that I was a fan of pizza and the Notorious B.I.G. and Bruce Springsteen, that I had at some point read at least *a* book, and that I performed stand-up comedy at some of America's ~~most illustrious, most storied, most renowned~~ venues.

In addition to our general awareness of one another, we'd also had a couple of public back-and-forth interactions and one brief DM (direct message, to those in the know, a.k.a. nerds who are online too much) exchange. I had tweeted that I was a little offended how often people recommended *Portnoy's Complaint* (Philip Roth's novel about an unpleasant Jewish guy who masturbates compulsively) to me. Maris had faved the tweet, which is a series of words that I understand is causing basically everyone over the age of sixty to search for the nearest well to throw this book down. Let's just say it's internet-speak for "she indicated that she enjoyed my joke." I then sent her a DM to thank her for acknowledging my Philip Roth reference, in hopes that she did not think that *I* was an unpleasant Jewish guy who masturbates compulsively.

So, that's the slightly wonky, slightly less classically romantic version of the story. We didn't "meet online" in the traditional sense of the phrase, but we did have a sporadic online correspondence before we met in person. But that's all complicated to explain to people who aren't regularly on the internet for personal or professional reasons. So we leave that part out depending on whom we're talking to. After that, it's basically the same as the short-and-sweet version.

Unless one of us tells you the rest of it.

The Whole Story

Here's the thing: nothing about the earlier versions of the story is false, or even misleading. The conversations were all accurately quoted. The emotional core of the events was not altered or embellished. Everything happened exactly as I related it. The one exception being, in reality it was way drunker.

I had already had a drink or two by the time I showed up at the party, which was unlike me. Years earlier, a headliner I was opening for asked me if I ever drank before my sets.

"I don't," I replied. "I don't really drink much at all."

"That's good," he said, before continuing, "I usually have two before I go on, and then I bring a third up with me. You don't want to have too many." He paused. "But God forbid you have too few." Those words stuck with me the way Hamlet remembered the dire proclamations of his father's ghost, a cautionary tale in seven words.

I showed up at Maris's get-together at Botanica, a Houston Street dive whose dim lighting didn't so much provide ambiance as plausible deniability of what the floors and seating would look like under direct light. Recognizing only Drew, the friend who invited me, and whom I also barely knew, I headed straight for the bar and ordered a cheap glass of terrible whiskey with enough ice to kill most of the taste. You don't want to deaden *all* the flavor, though, because otherwise you forget that it's poison and you drink it too fast. The trick is for the booze to taste bad enough that it cuts down on the danger of overconsumption. At least, I think that's how you're supposed to do it.

By the time I met Maris, she had a head start on me bever   agewise. I finished my first drink, which was really my third, and

I got another one, plus one for her in honor of her blog's anniversary.[3] We bullshitted and drank. Exuberant and, unbeknownst to us, three years from being married, we kissed at the bar, which by now you understand was not usually something I did. Not that I was opposed to making out with people immediately upon meeting them; it's that other people didn't often feel that way about me. In the past I usually needed more time to prove I'd be good to kiss and not just someone who could calculate the tip at a group dinner or help you jump-start your new boyfriend's car six months after we broke up. But it was happening that night. I was *being* fun. I was *having* fun. We were having fun.

As Maris and I talked more and kissed more, Drew sensed that our experience of the party no longer required more than just the two of us, and she began peeling other friends away, gently guiding them toward the door. She shepherded the stragglers out of the bar, and I had that same thought I'd had every time a woman showed interest in me: *Does this lady want me to take her home? Oh! Great!* Going back to her place would also avoid the embarrassment of her seeing my messy bedroom, which looked like burglars had trashed it looking for valuables, found none, and then trashed it further out of spite.

Maris paid her tab and we left the bar together. But in the cold late-night air and the hot wash of the streetlights it quickly became clear to me that Maris was a little tipsier than she'd seemed in the bar, a little wobbly on her feet in a way that hadn't regis-

---

3   Please feel free to give me a wedgie for writing that if you ever see me in public. I deserve it.

tered before. The situation presented a problem, because thanks to Drew's *Top Gun*–level wingwoman skills, there was no one else around.

My entire state of mind shifted. *Does this lady* need *me to take her home?* I thought. *Oh, great.* My life in a nutshell. Always the designated driver.

"I promise I'm not going to murder you," I said, like a murderer also would. "But it's late, and I want to make sure you get home safely. Do you live near here, at least?"

Without answering, Maris hailed a cab, crammed herself inside, and beckoned for me to join her. I figured I'd escort her the (presumably) short distance home, watch her safely enter her building, and then direct the cab driver onward to Harlem. The night was winding down at last.

The taxi driver asked Maris her address, and she gave him a pair of cross streets I'd never heard of. I pulled out my phone and Googled the names, which turned out to be in Brooklyn Heights, a cozy neighborhood on the Brooklyn waterfront, twenty minutes in the opposite direction from where I needed to go. Never mind. The night wasn't exactly young anymore, but it was still acting like it, like a white guy in his thirties who still used slang terms like "dope" and "lit."

When we got to Brooklyn, I asked Maris which building was hers, and I couldn't make out where she was pointing, so I paid the driver and got out of the car behind her to help complete the last leg of her journey. I'd never spent much time in Brooklyn Heights before. It wasn't cheap enough for most people I knew to be able to live there, and there weren't any comedy shows in the neighborhood that I was aware of, so I never really had an occasion to go. The streets all looked the same to me. Two- and three-story brownstones interspersed with a few larger buildings, none of them new, all of them distinguished, repeating themselves in a regularish pattern. It was like walking through a Hanna-Barbera cartoon remade by Wes Anderson. I hoped she knew where she was going.

"That's it!" Maris said. Her keys jangled for a while, like the intro to a Christmas carol, as she experimented to find the one that would open her front door. She swung the door open, and we hugged goodbye before she disappeared through the lobby.

I walked out toward the mainest street and waited a few minutes for another cab. *This is what the money's for*, I thought, like a just-recently-not-broke Don Draper. I got home shortly after one a.m., which I realize does not even crack the top ten million latest nights in New York City history. One in the morning in New York is like ten at night in most other American cities. People just expect you're willing to be up that late on any day of the week. Still, for a newly employed, historically unfun person, it counted as an adventure.

On top of that, I liked Maris right away. And, as I've gotten older, I've formed the opinion that if you like someone, you should tell them (unless you're married or they're married or they already told you they don't like you or they're a stranger on the bus or any other disqualifying circumstance arises). Playing it cool gets you nowhere. If you play it cool, and the other person plays it cool, then chances are you'll end up as two cool players who never kiss. Where's the fun in that? The worst thing that happens if you tell someone you're into them (a.k.a. "playing it hot") is that you find out they don't feel the same way about you. That is functionally the same as not doing anything and never finding out whether they are into you or not. Take your destiny into your own hands! Risk rejection for the sake of (potentially) finding love!

What that bravado looked like in action was a one p.m. text from my office. I tried to time it soon enough that I seemed on top of things, but not so fast that it seemed like I'd been lying awake, eyes wide open, waiting to talk to her.

> Hey you seemed like you were in some rough shape
> last night. Hope you're feeling better today.

Not my finest work, but it got the ball rolling. Maris wrote back that she was feeling, improbably, okay. I then texted her the second-coolest thing I've ever said, which was a considerable drop-off from the first.

> It was really great to meet you. Let's hang out
> sometime soon before it gets weird that we haven't
> hung out.

She agreed (hooray!), but between her work schedule and an upcoming trip out of town I had planned, there weren't many open windows for the two of us. We settled on a late breakfast (but still too early a meal to qualify as brunch) the following Saturday. I drove back to Brooklyn Heights, which was more charming in the daylight, when I wasn't exhausted and lost.

Because of the timing of our unconventional first real date, we were both clear eyed and alert. More than sober, we were fully caffeinated. Not that you need to drink for a date to be good, but the woozy glow of two drinks can help light the way toward a pleasant evening. (You don't want to have too many, but god forbid you have too few, after all.) On my ride to the restaurant I worried that maybe our daytime versions wouldn't be as compatible as our nighttime selves. There are some people who are fun to hang out with only when you're drunk, after all. Everyone has had friends whom you wouldn't go to a museum with and whose judgment you don't fully trust, but they're great for pounding booze, dancing, and talking shit. Conversely, there are also the friends you can *never* party with. Either they turn weird and dark, or they go too hard, forcing you to hit the eject button on the night after saying something like, "What? I didn't even know it was *possible* to take cocaine rectally!"

What if Maris liked only Party Josh, the Josh who had three drinks over four hours and invites you to Europe impulsively, even if he hopes you don't take him up on it, because it would be a little weird to meet his family that way? Scheduling the date felt like saying yes to a totally different kind of adventure than that earlier in the week, a high-focus, low-distraction situation in which I couldn't just duck out after ten minutes if things got weird.

To my great relief, we had a wonderful time eating omelets at a café before the brunch rush even started, like parents on vacation do. We talked about our new jobs and where we grew up. We drank iced coffee and resolved to see each other again soon. I don't remember if I kissed her goodbye,[4] but I do remember thinking, *Either way, it's going to be a little weird*, which it was, which was fine. And then I got in my car and drove to Rhode Island.

After that we dated for a year, in which time Maris saw my apartment exactly once. It was the Dorian Gray portrait of my recently much more stable life, and I didn't want her to see it, so I made the effort to visit her in Brooklyn, despite the distance. It was exactly the opposite of what I'd intended. We moved in together[5] and dated for another year before we got engaged. Then, a year after that, we got married. And now you know pretty much the whole story.

---

4   She says I did, and I believe her!
5   We always have sheets on the bed we share.

Fish Tacos

For years throughout high school, I carried around a can of chicken noodle soup to give to anyone I saw in the halls who seemed to be having a bad day. That seems, on its face, kind. But really what it was, was off-putting and bizarre. What is someone going to do with a can of chicken noodle soup in the middle of the school day? There's not even anywhere to heat it up. Plus, soup makes you feel better when you have a cold, not when you fail a test or get broken up with. I was performing generosity in a way that mostly cultivated an image of someone thoughtful and quirky. I was eccentric and boundaryless on purpose because I didn't have the confidence to be anything else.

I'd learned from movies and TV that the nerds were the good guys and the cool kids were the jerks. So I was careful to show that I knew my role in the school's ecosystem. I wasn't trendy, but boy was I *nice*.

By college, I had learned that friendship isn't a food drive, and I quit the schtick with the canned goods. But I still practiced food-based acts of affection. Although, as I've gotten busier and lazier, I've found that the threshold for cooking for others has become nearly insurmountably high. In fact, it's less of a threshold and more like one of those half doors that keeps horses in a barn while letting them look out at the farm. A trick I learned from my mom is that if you bring Chinese restaurant chicken fingers to a work potluck, people lose their minds. It blows your coworkers' pasta salads and salad-salads out of the water, and even though it feels like cheating, there's no rule against it. Still, when the occasion calls for it, I can slap together a pretty solid batch of brownies from a family recipe, but I save that for truly high-stakes events.

And when are the culinary stakes higher than in a new relationship?

For my fourth date with Maris, my now wife, I proposed that I would come over to her apartment and cook her dinner from scratch. I planned to make fish tacos because they don't require any elaborate preparation, but they show off a little more culinary range than the meals I usually prepared for myself: a big bowl of spaghetti, or a smaller bowl of spaghetti left over from the previous night's batch.

Cooking, I thought, would prove that I was domestic and planned ahead, two qualities Kate Hudson is always looking for in a man in movies. Maris was going to be so impressed. Unsure of what she had on hand, I bought all-new ingredients. A fresh canister of chili powder. A new bottle of olive oil. The tilapia, of course. I showed up laden with groceries and set to work.

After dinner, in true dude fashion, I felt disproportionately proud of my minor domestic accomplishment. That is, until Maris ever so gently let me know that while she appreciated my gesture, she didn't really like fish. And, more important, Maris has diabetes and tortillas aren't great for her blood sugar. I probably should have done a little more research before dinner. I could have—at the very least—asked a few basic questions like, "Is this food something you'd ever voluntarily eat?" and "Could this dinner accidentally murder you?"

A surprise is worthwhile only if it's something the other person actually enjoys. Otherwise you're just saying, "Here you go! Please pretend to like this for the sake of my self-esteem!"

Fish tacos, which I chose because they were easy and fake sophisticated, were pretty much the worst possible choice. Not only did she not like them, they were actively terrible for her health. I'm glad I hadn't also baked brownies. It would have seemed like a low-key assassination attempt.

From that night on, I have always asked Maris what *she* wants for dinner before launching into some elaborate preparation (or, far more often, ordering takeout).

In five years, her answer has never once been fish tacos.

Tickle Me Fancy

I don't remember the specific moment I fell in love with Maris, but I can pinpoint the exact second I realized I wanted to be with her always. It was sixteen hours after we buried my grandmother, and Maris and I were lying in bed at my parents' house. Technically, we were lying in beds. We lay side by side on two twin mattresses, nestled together in a single frame. It was an apparatus my parents inherited from my mother's parents, who slept like that for as long as I can remember, an arrangement I've never heard of before or since.

The day had felt like three. We'd woken up early to attend the funeral, at which I spoke. As the member of my immediate family most comfortable with public and public-adjacent speaking, I have given eulogies at several of my grandparents' funerals. It's a way I'm specifically qualified to contribute, and it helps me locate myself in the mosaic of my extended family. I take the responsibility of eulogizing seriously, as if there were any other way to take it, so I'd been up late the night before, trying to sum up my grandmother's life in eight hundred words.

The burden of sadness squashed down on top of me, compressed by the additional weight of conveying Nana Kay's vast personality. A woman of precise and far-ranging taste, she'd traveled to all seven continents and somehow returned with hideous, unwearable souvenirs as gifts for me and my sister. Even into her late eighties, she remained a matriarch of impressive gravity. She drove. She baked. She argued. Two weeks before her funeral, she had essentially hosted Thanksgiving dinner from her deathbed. She slept through the festivities, family congregated nearby. I stayed up late, typing and erasing, struggling with the words to summarize her the next morning in front of those who knew her best.

The ceremony was held at a Jewish cemetery, despite Nana Kay's staunch secularity. In fact, she'd wrangled special permission from a rabbi to be cremated, despite the general Jewish prohibition on the practice. Even in death, she made sure things were just the way she wanted. I delivered the eulogy after brief speeches by my cousin Amy and my great-aunt Barbara, Kay's sister. Afterward, we hugged and cried, which I think means I did an okay job.

From the cemetery, we had gone straight to my parents' living room, where we spent the afternoon sitting shiva. Shiva is the Jewish tradition of spending the days after the passing of a loved one surrounded by friends and family. It was comforting to spend the afternoon around the cousins I see only when someone dies, eating the kind of deli platter I see only when someone dies. I've had corned beef at my parents' house six times total, always following the death of a relative.

It was the first time Maris had met most of my family, and a funeral wasn't the *ideal* circumstance for light introductions, but where else are you going to meet a third cousin? A wedding, I guess, but that's even worse. At least at a funeral you get fewer questions about when "you two are going to tie the knot."

That evening, as cousins had begun to trickle out of the house, Maris and I borrowed my mom's Prius to go into Boston. I'd had a few stand-up shows scheduled that night, and I didn't want to cancel them, because I get stressed out backing out of obligations, and also because doing comedy helps me feel like myself. It's not that what I say onstage is like therapy. Generally, I think comedians who claim that comedy is "like therapy" for them are bad at either comedy, therapy, or both. But I started stand-up when I was nineteen, and I do it most nights, so it feels routine to go out to a show, the way that if you have an office job, it can make you feel normal to go to an office. *Here I am at work, life going on the way it does, and such.* I didn't want to be Family Me anymore. I wanted to put on jeans and take a break from explaining internet things to people in their seventies.

We hopped in the car and, having no other music option, turned on the radio, and the first song we heard was "Caress Me Down" by the band Sublime. Sublime is not a good band. They're like a skateboard that you listen to. They are, in my experience, taken *very* seriously by people from California, much like the Red Hot Chili Peppers, fresh avocados, and the low-grade fear of being swept into the sea by an earthquake. "Caress Me Down" specifically is a very bad song. And yes, it's a cover, but they do it very Sublimely.

Maris started singing along with the radio, and I couldn't stop laughing. What did me in was the impassioned performance of the lyric "Kiss me neck and tickle me fancy!" (A line that sounds innocuous on its own but is part of a run of almost-rhymes that includes the word "horny." Gross! Keep "horny" out of your song lyrics![1] "Horny" is a word for drunk text messages only, IF THAT.)

The commitment with which Maris bellowed the line cracked me up, and it made the day a little less gloomy. We bounced between the three shows, which I will not describe in detail, because describing a stand-up show is *barely* more tolerable than describing an improv show, which is *barely* more tolerable than describing a dream.

By the time the last show wrapped up, it was after midnight, and we'd been fully *on* since nine in the morning. For the moment, exhaustion smothered the grief. We got back in the Prius and headed back to my parents' house. When the radio came on, the first song we heard was *once again* "Caress Me Down" by Sublime, which was jarring. The song was, at the time, sixteen years old and had never even been released as a single. Hearing it twice by chance within a few hours felt like some kind of wizard's curse. *What terrible fate is about to befall us?* I wondered.

This time, we joined the song in medias res, at the Spanish part. Maris, not knowing Spanish, but refusing to back down from her earlier bit, did an enthusiastic, fist-shaking dance at me, as if I'd just denied her a mortgage or dinged her car while pulling out

---

1   The one exception: "Pony" by Ginuwine.

of a parking spot. Again I laughed. It was very kind of her to give such a full-throttle performance of such a terrible song, all for my benefit. I loved her very much.[2]

We arrived home just before one in the morning, depleted. We tiptoed up the creaky stairs, peeled off our cold-weather clothes, and burrowed under the covers. I lay on my left side with my right arm draped over Maris's body across the crease where the two twin mattresses met. I didn't intend to pass out like that. It is, at least for the two of us, impossible to sleep while spooning. It's a fiction from romantic movies, the same as falling in love with your greatest business rival or meeting your soul mate after she spills a cauldron of soup (charmingly!) onto your computer. But that night, wrung out of emotion and energy, I had started to drift into sleep while snuggled tightly against Maris, relieved to have made it through the day, and nervous about the wellspring of feeling that awaited me in the morning. I feared the turbulence that lurked beneath the busyness and tiredness.

"Josh," she whispered, so gently, so sweetly, her voice like a snowflake landing on a dog's nose. "Kiss my neck?"

And in that moment (and of course in many moments since) I would have done anything for her, whatever I could do to make her life easier and more comfortable. Kiss her neck. Scratch her back. Rub her feet. Whatever she needed, she'd been so wonderful to me all day under such stressful circumstances, and I was ready to pay her back.

I curled toward her to plant the tiniest, tenderest kiss on the

---

2   And also I still do.

back of her neck. And as I did, she turned to face me, making eye contact with one eye, like a hammerhead shark.

"AND TICKLE ME FANCY!" she blurted out. She Sublimed me. In my childhood bedroom. On the day of my grandmother's funeral.

And I don't know what they call that where you're from, but in Stoneham, Massachusetts, that's called a keeper.

A Good Game

I spent the first February night of 2015 huddled with friends around a disproportionately large television in a tiny Brooklyn living room watching the Super Bowl. The game was close, but the nerves I felt on account of the Patriots' evaporating lead were coagulating into a thick, bigger-than-sports sadness.

Not again.

That was the text my dad sent me after Jermaine Kearse, the Seahawks' receiver, bobbled the ball over his entire body like a contact juggler before holding on to it inside the Patriots' ten-yard line. My stomach pitched and lurched. I sank down into the couch like loose change.

"Hey, this might sound weird," I said to the party, "but however this game ends, I think I'm going to start crying. My grandmother died. I'll explain after."

It was embarrassing to admit to a room full of cosmopolitan

New York writers and media professionals (in other words, non-townies) who felt more vicarious embarrassment for Katy Perry's rhythmless Left Shark[1] than attachment to any football team. Nobody expected to be in the presence of an actual Sports Maniac, the kind of person whose happiness depends on the score of a game played thousands of miles away. Until that fall, I hadn't even known I was one of those people.

And then Nana Kay, my last surviving grandparent, got sick. Well, she'd been sick, but in October we found out what it was. The pain in her legs, which had grown unbearable around her eighty-ninth birthday, wasn't arthritis; it was lymphoma. Suddenly, she needed twenty-four-hour care from her three children, which my father and his siblings dutifully provided in shifts, even after she was admitted to Newton-Wellesley Hospital outside Boston.

Although my grandmother was a strict parent and abided my grandfather's kosher diet, as a nana she had grown away from religion and was almost unbelievably permissive (unbelievable primarily to my father, who had known her as a mom). She participated in my bar mitzvah, proudly, but with no sense of comfort or familiarity around the Torah.

On the other hand, a few years earlier, I'd given her a recording of a stand-up comedy show I'd done. "There's some adult material on here, and if you have any questions about what it means . . . never talk to me about it," I said.

A week later I got a one-sentence email (a feat in itself) from her. It was brief and sarcastic: "Oh, I get it."

---

1   A wildly dated but completely apt reference.

She'd been so healthy up until her diagnosis that the doctors spoke of her condition in terms of "full recovery" rather than "years, months, or days left." Still, the time in the hospital wore on her. She was used to being independent; she'd been retired less than a decade, working into her eighties doing patient billing for hospitals to finance her trips to all seven continents.

When you're confined to a hospital bed, there aren't many appointments you can make. You await visits from friends and family members. You enjoy the coconut ice cream they smuggle in. You tolerate the erratic and invasive visits of doctors and nurses, hoping that one of them will bring you closer to going home. But you don't have a lot of control over your social calendar. During my grandmother's hospital stay, the NFL schedule became the one event she could make an appointment for herself. Physical therapy and visits from cousins came according to the whims of everyone around her. Patriots games were her time.

"I wish I'd been able to stay up and watch the second half," she told me with a sigh over the phone the morning after one game, the frustration with her illness boiled down to a single point of practical concern.

Before Nana Kay was diagnosed with cancer, I thought I was done with the NFL entirely. I had walked away, and I had no regrets. Between the league's dismal handling of domestic violence issues to its resistance to effectively addressing the brain injuries sustained by its players, I couldn't watch a game with a clear conscience. Also, the Patriots looked bad. Like, really bad. Smoked 41–14 in late September by the lowly Kansas City Chiefs on *Monday Night Football* bad.

It was disappointing because I had a long history as a fan. In 1986, my dad squeezed infant me into a "Squish the Fish" T-shirt for good luck . . . right before the Patriots got crushed by the Bears. I'd celebrated the team's three Super Bowl wins and agonized over the three losses in the big game. Where I'm from, this qualifies as "casually following" a team. I wouldn't call myself a "bro," but I would say I'm a "hardened twerp." Plus, kickoff always reminded me to at least text my dad.

Honestly, I had never really thought of my grandmother as a sports fan; the rest of her personality was too vibrant and far ranging to be defined that way. Kay Gondelman was adventurous and candid and acerbic and giving. She always brought family members a souvenir from her latest trip to Asia, but she never hesitated to tell someone how the birthday gift they'd gotten her had missed the mark. During the summer of 2011, as I was preparing to move from Boston to New York, I took my grandmother out to lunch. Afterward we went back to her apartment, where she had baked a cake for dessert. We sat at her dining room table and talked about everything you're not supposed to talk about with a grandparent. Abortion, religion, even (*gasp*) Israel. She told me, for the first time, how she hadn't believed in God for decades. She couldn't believe that a benevolent force would allow the horrors of the world (I don't need to list them here) to persist.

It was comforting to hear her thoughts, because I've never felt attached to Judaism in any traditional way. I'm not religious. But I'm also not spiritual. I used to drive home from New York to Boston for Yom Kippur and Passover at my mother's request, but over the years, my motivation to make those trips has dwindled. At this

point, the most Jewish thing about me is that I still love the Beastie
Boys. I appreciate how central religion can be in the lives of other
people, but it has never resonated with me. I imagine this is how
lots of people feel about things I love, like rap music or, it turns
out, sports.

I didn't quite realize how important the Patriots were to Kay's
life until I got a text from my mother near the end of October
saying she'd delayed a cancer treatment to guarantee she'd feel
well enough to watch the Pats play. That is, in my estimation, the
strongest possible commitment to a sports team. Forget waking
up at five thirty to tailgate or even getting a mascot tattooed on
your ankle. There is no more impressive show of team spirit than
postponing chemotherapy to watch a game. Tears crept down my
cheeks as I sat, overwhelmed by my grandmother's commitment to
living her life exactly as she chose even in spite of her own doctors.

She started chemo the next day, but it didn't take. The doctors were able to manage the pain, but there were complications,
and those complications interrupted the treatment, and the cancer spread. But the NFL season continued unhindered. By this
time, whatever moral high ground I'd taken against the NFL had
eroded. While my job in New York kept me physically distant from
my grandmother most of the time, keeping track of football gave
us something to talk about on the phone. Watching ESPN high-
light packages gave me the comfort I imagine people derive from
murmuring a prayer over rosary beads.

When I visited in November, I brought a Tom Brady jersey.
My father duct-taped it to the wall of the hospital room. I told her
about my plans for the time off over the holidays.

"I'm going to finish writing my book."

"Yeah, I've heard you say that a lot," she replied.

By the time I came home for Thanksgiving, the doctors had given up on the chemo and sent my grandmother home. My family ate Thanksgiving dinner at her house as we always did, but she wasn't well enough to leave her bedroom. I sat with her before returning to New York.

"I love you," I said.

"I love you," she whispered. I squeezed her hand and walked toward the door.

"Don't party too hard!" I called to her over my shoulder, which I maintain was a pretty solid bit.

She died the following Monday. My mom called to tell me, and I stoically made plans to return for the funeral. An hour later, I got a text saying that my grandmother was going to be cremated with the Tom Brady jersey. Then I cried, thinking that if she hadn't just died, my grandmother could be elected mayor of Boston on that platform alone. I later joked to my parents that I couldn't control my tears because I'd paid like a hundred dollars for that shirt. I think she would have appreciated it. But really I was crying because the shirt and the team it represented hadn't provided a strong enough foothold against the relentless current of her illness.

So two months later, when the Seahawks seemed poised to clinch an improbable Super Bowl victory, everything felt so unfair. Nana Kay's death, but also the score of the game itself. Don't you accrue some kind of sports karma when you are laid to rest, ashes intermingled with officially licensed team apparel? Does such fidelity mean nothing? And then, when Malcolm Butler jumped a route and intercepted Russell Wilson's pass over the middle, re-claiming the game for the Patriots, I was overwhelmed by how unfair everything still felt. My grandmother, who showed unbe-lievable devotion to her team, missed its most thrilling moment, which was even *more* unfair than if they'd lost. Of course it felt bad. Any result would have probed the wound of the loss of Nana Kay. No football score could have erased it.

Even in my excitement over the result of the Super Bowl, I didn't feel like my grandmother was present or watching over me. I felt her absence in an acute, urgent, painful way. Because she *wasn't* present. She was dead, and she'd missed out on something that would have brought her a lot of joy. Tears leaked down my face on the long subway ride home. I realized I might never be able to watch football again without missing her. I realized that might be a good thing. Despite its flaws, the NFL has given me a wonderful gift of remembrance, which is how I imagine a lot of people feel about religion.

I quit the NFL a second time after that Super Bowl. It's not like my grandmother's death had solved the structural problems with the league.[2] Then team owners started to crack down when players like Colin Kaepernick began using the playing of the na-tional anthem as an opportunity to kneel in silent protest of police violence against people of color. And, of course, there was the pub-lic friendship between then-candidate Donald Trump and Tom Brady, Bill Belichick, and Bob Kraft (the Patriots' star quarterback, head coach, and team owner, respectively).

---

2   Although imagine if it had!

It had become somehow even *less* acceptable to root for the Patriots, an endeavor which, even before 2016, felt a little like watching *Beauty and the Beast* and cheering for Gaston. Yes, he has a perfect butt-chin, and maybe you grew up cheering for him, but come on. He's a pitchfork-wielding vigilante who probably already has the small French village equivalent of five Super Bowl rings.

And it was not just more frowned upon, it was also less appealing to cheer for the Pats, too. It almost seemed like a dare, as the reasons to abandon both the sport in general and the team specifically piled up. As the 2016 season continued, I felt sure that someday soon photos of Charles Manson with a Patriots logo prison stick-and-poke tattoo were going to emerge.

So, in the weeks leading up to the 2016 presidential election, I once again jumped ship on professional football, which was easy. There was almost no reason to watch. And at the time, my job kept me in the office on Sunday afternoons, when most NFL games are played, so even casually enjoying the season would have been a hassle.

But then, as fall became winter, the Patriots once again marched their way toward the Super Bowl behind the arm of Tom Brady, which was still as true and unerring as his friendship with a certain casino failure/reality star/POTUS was public and unnerving. When I read his blithe explanation for the Make America Great Again hat he had in his locker in late 2015, it made me want to uncremate my grandmother, or at least sift the jersey out of her ashes somehow. And it's like, how dare this handsome, square-jawed goober remind me so much of Nana Kay? The nerve of him.

Every slight felt like a desecration of my grandmother's memory. But I couldn't stop thinking about her death, and so I couldn't stop thinking about the Patriots.

Once again I was sucked back in, the looming Patriots Super Bowl appearance and its now-complicated connection to my family history pulled me back to football, the way defensive coverage warps to account for the unignorable presence of Pro Bowl tight end Rob Gronkowski.[3] And yes, that makes me a fair-weather fan, but in my defense, sports teams are the only sources of entertainment we're supposed to support even when they're bad. No one calls you a fair-weather picnicker if you refuse to spread out a blanket and eat sandwiches in the rain. No one doubts your love of science fiction if you don't know the script to John Travolta's debacle *Battlefield Earth* verbatim.

By the time of Donald Trump's inauguration in January 2017, I had decided to go home to Massachusetts to watch the Super Bowl with my family. Still, I was besieged by a full-on blitz of emotions: despair for the state of the country, painful/joyful remembrance of Nana Kay, and a grudging yet undeniable excitement for the game itself. I had no idea how to reconcile those feelings. It's weird that a human brain can experience them all at once, like an unsettling piano chord played by a cat hopping onto a keyboard. The notes don't "go together," per se, but they're definitely happening at the same time.

I posted about my ambivalence on Facebook, along with the conclusion that maybe if I donated a little money to causes that

---

3   I also hate how easily this analogy came to me.

fought against the president's racist, sexist, transphobic agenda, it might do more good than any harm I'd be perpetrating by cheering for the team I'd been brought up to love. My friend Emma suggested that it was likely other people felt the same way, and that we could form a campaign suggesting they donate, too. We decided on the hashtag #AGoodGame as a way to encourage other people to donate and track their donations.

We got three responses to the campaign online:

1. "Cool! I'd love to be a part of that!"

2. "Your [sic] a pussy. You shouldn't even watch football if you don't like it."

   (Which is silly. People do things they have qualms with all the time. Life is full of deciding when to make compromises and when to take hard-line stances. If you can make a clean, immediate break with every institution that gives you a moment's moral hesitation, you are rare and admirable. And also, most likely, you are insufferable at parties.)

3. "Why not make a statement by refusing to watch the game?"

I grappled with the third point, with limited success. The immediate but unsatisfying response was "I want to watch the game." In part, the fund-raiser served to back-justify that decision, which would have been enough if the question had been just about me.

But in a more substantial way, appealing to the consciences of people who were going to watch the game anyway seemed like the best way to do the most good.

It's very hard to get people to *not* do something they're intent on doing. An effort to boycott the Super Bowl would have made a negligible effect on the ratings (and that's being generous). And, considering the difficulty standing *against* the NFL, it made sense to activate people's desire to stand *for* something. No one's individual viewership would make or break the National Football League. Anyone's individual donation could help the NAACP or the ACLU (or any of the other myriad charities people chose as their cause). But also, my grandmother was dead, and if watching football once a year was an inextricable part of my long-term grieving, then so be it.

My dad picked me up at South Station a few hours before the game began and brought me back to my parents' house, where my entire family camped out in front of the television. As the first half unfolded, the Atlanta Falcons had begun, for lack of a better term, beating the ever-living shit out of the Patriots. The score sat at 28–3 (in favor of Atlanta) as Lady Gaga began her halftime performance, which is not an auspicious football score. At least it didn't get worse before the time the second half began. Gaga didn't somehow manage to torch the Pats' cornerbacks for a long touchdown on a post route.

The night, to that point, had felt like a joke at my expense. I'd neatly triangulated a way to manage my warring family and football and political emotions, only to watch my team get smushed into the turf by their opponents. It was a fresh kind of anguish I had not anticipated. *Let this be a lesson to me,* I thought, *about trying to have your cake and eat it, too.* Losing felt even worse than winning had two years before. That's usually how that goes.

Most Super Bowls are not especially competitive football games. So I didn't anticipate a comeback. At best, I hoped that the Patriots would put up a few points in garbage time for the benefit of the charities people had pledged money to. Then the improbable happened, which you know if you follow sports at all and don't care about if you don't. I'll spare you the play-by-play, but the Patriots clawed their way back into a competitive game, taking it to overtime.

The #AGoodGame hashtag was full of jubilant New Englanders and flustered Patriots haters. People donated in amounts as low as $1 a point or as high $100 per touchdown. When all was said and done, we learned, thanks to Emma's expert data analysis, that over $100,000 had been donated, which felt satisfying and encouraging. But in the moment, I felt defiant and righteous, like Diddy and Nas wearing crowns of thorns in the video for the song "Hate Me Now," which is kind of a deep cut, but you can Google it.

When the Pats pushed the game into overtime and eventually won, I thought of my grandmother and cried again. What the fuck, football? It is illogical and infuriating that twenty-two guys running into each other on a field can be so evocative of the memory of a woman who had never even played the game. And yet, that's how it was. And that's probably how it always will be.

When the Patriots *again* made it to the Super Bowl the following year, Emma and I revived the #AGoodGame drive. I took the

Amtrak home to Massachusetts to watch the game with my family. When they lost to the Eagles, I felt disappointment in the team, happiness for the people of Philadelphia, connection to Nana Kay, pride at raising money, and dread at the prospect of waking up at five thirty to take the train to New York in time for work. It never gets less complicated, I guess.

The Patriots won the Super Bowl again in 2019, and the feelings (as well as the fundraising effort) came back. Nana Kay has been gone for more than four years now, but the heightened tension of the big game always makes me think of her. I swear I don't know if my heart will be able to handle it if Tom Brady doesn't retire soon. But unfortunately, it'll probably also wreck me when he does.

The Unsung Virtue of Telling People What They Want to Hear

Hotel lonely is a special kind of lonely. It's not just solitary; it's unfamiliar, too. You're not used to the shower's water pressure or the mattress's firmness. Even the order of the TV channels is unfamiliar. *TNT comes right before Fox? I am a long way from home.* But ultimately it's the solitude that's the worst. It makes you do weird things.

There are plenty of songs about life on the road, mostly classic rock songs, unless I've failed to grasp the subtext of some jazz. But I never related to those songs, because I don't have children to miss, and I don't do cocaine, and most of the songs mention being very successful and having throngs of adoring fans, which seems a *little* braggy to me.

When you pare away all the famous trappings of life on the road, you're left with fast food, travel delays, masturbation (not mentioned explicitly in most of the songs, but a central part of the experience nonetheless), and accidentally packing too few undergarments. Whenever I accidentally step in a puddle of water next to the bathtub at a Holiday Inn Express and have to pull off a wet sock I sing to myself, "There I goooooooo . . . turn the paaaaaage."

At least when you're in a touring band, there are other people around to hang out with or fistfight (if you're in Oasis) or get married to and/or cheat on your spouse with (if you're in Fleetwood Mac). As a comic on the road, you're often alone or working with people with whom you have nothing in common. Personally, I was rarely interested in finding an audience member to sleep with and was never concerned with finding a local to buy drugs from, so I occasionally disqualified myself from my peers' late-night activities. Usually after my sets, I ended up back at the hotel room, where it was too early for bed but too late to pretend I was going to use the gym.

Still, the classic rock wisdom about the postperformance feeling holds true: if the show went well, you want to keep that high going. If the show went badly, you want to cheer yourself up. That's the common explanation for why so many performers suffer with substance abuse. Drugs, from what I've heard, can make you feel good until they very much don't.

After a rough breakup in 2012, I had a long stretch of shows booked out of town, and I was dreading the late hotel nights, not just alone, but with no one to even text goodnight. To insulate myself from myself, I started a blog in which I promised to write a postcard to anyone who asked me for one. I got over three hundred requests, which took me a year and over a hundred dollars in postage to complete. By the end, it got a little annoying to scribble out vague messages to strangers, but annoyed was better than despondent.

After I finished my postcard project, my go-to move to feel like part of society while on the road became Twitter Pep Talks. Twitter, which I've mentioned in previous chapters, is a social network that C-list celebrities use to complain about airlines, and white supremacists use to try to ruin the careers and threaten the lives of women, people of color, and Jews in media. But also, lots of regular nonmonsters use it to talk with friends and keep abreast of breaking news and avoid admitting they've aged into the Facebook demographic.

On a professional level, I have trouble writing Twitter off entirely. The viral Modern Seinfeld Twitter account that my friend Jack Moore and I cocreated was an embarrassingly strong kick in the ass of my career. If you don't know what that is (and why would you?), Jack and I wrote 140-character pitches for episodes of *Seinfeld*, were it still on the air. The account accrued about 800,000 followers, including some people within show business, and it opened a lot of doors for the two of us. And personally, Twitter is (kind of) where I met my wife. I owe a lot to Twitter, which is humiliating. It's as if I found a hundred dollars at the bottom of an open sewer I'd fallen into and then later I fell in again and found a diamond ring, so I have a lingering fondness for that particular sewer despite the rats and human waste that it exists to facilitate.

Technically, I didn't start doing Twitter Pep Talks on the road. The first time I offered them was the night of a canceled gig in New Haven. A promoter had offered me a couple hundred dollars to headline a show in Connecticut, which fell through on the day it was supposed to happen. Emotionally speaking, the timing couldn't have been worse. I'd spent that whole year writing submission materials for various TV shows and not getting jobs. I had

booked a stand-up set on a late-night TV show, and they post-
poned my appearance because the network thought my material
was "too dark." Then, in the wake of that, I sold a piece of writing
to a prestigious magazine, which was squashed by an editor the
day it was supposed to run online. And on top of all that, I couldn't
even do a fucking gig in Connecticut that was barely worth the
cost of gas and tolls to get there in the first place.

When the show disintegrated on account of low ticket sales
because "the website went down" and also "nobody in New Haven had any idea who I was," it pile-drove[1] me through the flimsy
folding table of my previous self-esteem low onto what I assumed
was the floor of my confidence.[2] I felt professionally adrift and un-
accomplished, convinced that what I'd achieved to date was all
I would ever be capable of. A mentally healthier (but physically
the same, *at best*) version of me can look back on that period and
realize it wasn't that I was hitting the ceiling of my potential; I was
on the verge of breaking through a wall—but there was no way to
know that at the time. On the plus side, the producer promised

---

1 Pile-drived? That can't be right. I've never heard the past tense of that verb,
   probably because wrestlers are so good at living in the moment.

2 It wasn't! My honest-to-goodness career low came a month later, when I
   took my girlfriend to see *Inside Llewyn Davis*. If you haven't seen the movie,
   here is a brief synopsis: Oscar Isaac plays a New York City–based folk singer,
   who is medium talented but also a monumental asshole, who ruins every
   personal and professional relationship in his life in pursuit of stardom. He
   fails because he is medium talented and also a colossal asshole. *That is me,*
   I thought while watching that movie. *That is my destiny.* I was sure of it,
   despite the obvious differences between me and that character. I am not a
   folk singer. I am not a *monumental* asshole. And I do not have Oscar Isaac's
   bone structure or hairline.

to PayPal me the money for the New Haven show anyway. Conversely, he didn't. (If you're reading this, I'm on Venmo now! You blew me off so long ago that there's new technology! But the offer for you to give me $200 still stands!)

The first time I offered pep talks online was the night of my canceled Connecticut gig. I was at home and feeling low. When I opened Twitter, my initial impulse was to ask the internet for help. I wanted to hear a kind word or two. But, ugh, that seemed so *needy*. And things weren't *that bad*. Thanks to a patchwork of freelance gigs (tutoring, stand-up, magazine writing), I had enough money to pay my bills. I had lots of great friends I could turn to in a crisis. I am, despite my tendency to miss birthdays and weddings for work commitments, reasonably good at keeping in touch via text message. I wasn't even suffering from depression. I was just . . . bummed out.

Solitary and needy, I wondered: What if instead of asking for something, I offered something instead? That way, I'd still get to hear kind words, with the caveat that I would be the one saying those kind words. And maybe that would help other people a little bit, which would, in turn, make me feel better. I'm generally in favor of doing things for others as a means to feeling better about myself. There's a limit to how much I can complain before it starts to make me feel worse. The inverse is not true. There's no amount of volunteer work you can do that will make you think, *Oh, no. I'm a monster.*

My first pep talk offer got about thirty requests, a mixture of friends and strangers, all of whom I answered as specifically as I could.

"You are a [sic] smart and successful while remaining creative and generous," I replied to an acquaintance.

"You rock a tasteful level of stubble and dope shades," I tweeted, like a dweeb, to someone whose photo featured a tasteful level of stubble and stylish sunglasses.

The pep talks did, in fact, make me feel better. It was like an instant, straight-to-the-vein version of my postcards. I felt plugged into a community, and it was really heartwarming that people were comfortable indulging my awkward and tender premise. And my tweets seemed to make other people feel better, too. Over the past several years, I've kept doing the pep talks, usually when I'm in a hotel after a show, wired or moderately despondent, depending on how it went. It always improves my night, even on the evenings when I nod off midpep and have to finish in the morning.

Probably the most valuable thing I've learned from years of encouraging friends and strangers on the internet is the value of telling people what they want to hear. Obviously, there are exceptions to this rule. Giving someone only positive feedback when they really need some tough love is like letting a child maintain a gummy bears–only diet because you don't want to deal with the tantrums that come with forcing him to eat broccoli. Sure, you're avoiding a little interpersonal strife, but translucent colors are not the same as food groups! That baby will grow up to have no teeth and squishy bones!

There are some extenuating circumstances that make certain encouragements ring hollow. Blithe cheerleading isn't a substitute for therapy or antidepressants or having enough money to pay rent. People suffering from depression can't just hear "You're doing great!" and go, "Oh yeah. What was I thinking? I *am* doing great!" And the obstacles many people are up against in terms of institutional racism, sexism, and other prejudices make many goals harder to achieve than they would be in a more just world. So I realize that as a straight, white, neurotypical, cisgender man with a modest savings account, I need to be extra considerate of others' experiences. Otherwise, I could easily sound like the frat guy of guys who was never in a fraternity: "Bummer you got that DUI and wrecked your Lambo, brah. Now you have to ask your dad to buy you a new car."

Still, I maintain that telling people what they want to hear under most circumstances is, as my grandmother would say "a mitzvah," or as Martha Stewart would less Jewishly call it, "a good thing." And yes, it's hard to know what that means to any specific person, especially when that person is an internet stranger whose bio is brief quotes from *Mean Girls* or *Twin Peaks*, and whose timeline is full of retweets from progressive politicians. Sometimes a person's message to me is something general, like "I could really use some pep, please!"

Here are a few general things that people like to hear and are often true:

- As bad as things feel right now, they can get better with time and effort.

- You are not alone. There are people in your life who are there for you and want to help.

- You are already excellent, and you're not done getting better.

There are very few problems to which those answers are not generally true and at least pleasant to hear. Yes, there are people who are truly alone, who have no one to reach out to for help. And sure, some people are vile Dumpster dwellers who are terrible now and are actively trying to get worse, so they do not deserve to be told they are excellent. I think, though, that the former group is rare, and the latter group is not inclined to ask a stranger for encouragement. They're more likely to say to themselves (or others): "It's weird how I'm so awesome but everyone still hates me. That seems wrong. Everyone who's not me is so dumb."

Sometimes the questions are more specific. Here are a few more I often get, and variations on the respective pep talk I reply with.

- I have a job interview tomorrow, and I'm nervous.
  Unless you fabricated *massive* stretches of your résumé, they called you in because they like you, and all you have to do is be you in the interview.

- This week is crazy with finals/work/family obligations/home renovation, and I don't know how I'll get through it.
  It'll be hard, but you'll do it, and then it'll be done forever.

- The world . . . it's so bad.
  The world may seem like a shit volcano constantly erupting diarrhea into a fart-clouded sky, but lots of people are working hard to improve it, and you can be one of them.

This is of course not a substitute for activism or advocacy or charity. It does not make me a good person. There are plenty of people who are cheerful and encouraging while also being creeps or war profiteers or, I imagine, horse thieves. But I have the good fortune to get to travel around the country saying nonsense as a significant part of my career. It's like eating pizza for a job. It's fun, and I'm lucky to do it, but it's probably not *good* for me. To me, the pep talks are like eating salad. It's a little thing I can do in addition to all the pizza to make sure my body continues to operate. Because as an adult, I accept that I cannot live on pizza alone.

And look, sometimes it's late at night and I've had one or maybe two drinks. And I'm overthinking everything that brought me to wherever I am, one hundred, or three hundred, or three thousand miles away from my wife, who is definitely asleep. Or maybe I'm right next to her and she fell asleep early, and I'm wondering what the heck I'm doing with my life anyway. Maybe I'm in a hotel room with sheets that feel like butcher paper and an air conditioner that fires up with a sound like a Transformer turning from bus to fightin' robot every forty-five minutes. Maybe the shades don't close all the way, and headlights from the highway outside strobe through the crack at all hours, so it feels like you're sleeping in a discotheque or a science museum. At times like those it is nice to be able to offer something to other people, no matter how paltry it seems. And hopefully they think it's nice, too.

An Element of Style

I unexpectedly became a sneakerhead a few years ago. If you're unfamiliar with the term, I realize it sounds like a lesser-known Dick Tracy villain, but it's serious shoe collector slang for a serious shoe collector. It started at Carolines on Broadway, the Manhattan comedy club where I was opening for my friend Ron Funches. He and Yassir Lester,[1] the other comic on the bill, had such good sneakers. They were clean and bright and coordinated with their outfits. And I, wearing the last of my long line of identical pairs of Saucony Jazz running shoes, felt jealous.

I wasn't jealous of Yassir's and Ron's *specific* shoes, so much as the idea of having a distinctive personal style. Working with them made me realize, "Oh yeah. You can wear shoes for other reasons than 'they don't hurt my feet' or 'they were on sale.'" *Maybe I can be that kind of person*, I thought. I dress fine, not great. Nobody would

---

1   Yassir also has a sneaker-centric podcast called *My Brother's Sneaker* that he hosts with his brother Isaiah. It is very funny and informative!

copy my look, but I am also unlikely to be ambushed by five benevolent gay men ready to make me over on television. *Maybe from the ankles down I can get comfortable being noticed*, I thought, excited but anxious as being seen as a late adopter or, more bluntly, a tool.[2]

I've always worn sneakers, but for most of my life my rotation stayed between one and three pairs. The shoes I wore most of the time, the older beat-up pair that I'd wear in inclement weather or to a park, and the ones I'd pretend I was going to work out in. But as the weekend wrapped up, I decided that the next occasion I had to celebrate, I'd buy my own pair of statement sneakers.

The following week I had the silly good fortune to be nominated for an Emmy.[3] I went out and bought a pair of forest green–neon pink Jordan 1s (the model that Michael Jordan wore during his rookie season in the NBA). They were not especially comfortable, but I liked wearing them just the same. They felt bold and out of character, and as I walked around in the stiff, un-broken-in retros, they served as a tactile reminder that I was an *Emmy nominee*.

Since then, I've marked basically every major life milestone with a new pair of shoes. I bought myself a pair when my most recent stand-up album came out. I've purchased sneakers to wear for TV appearances and to award shows. I got a fresh pair of black-and-red floral-patterned Kevin Durant signature low-tops to wear with my tuxedo for my wedding reception.

---

2   In fairness, my footwear had been commented on in the past. My (very funny!) comedian friend Noré Davis used to call me "Boardwalk Shoes" because a pair of hideous dress shoes I sometimes wore reminded him of the show *Boardwalk Empire*.

3   I lost.

It happened slowly, but wearing flashy sneakers stopped feeling out of character for me and started feeling like "a thing I do." It was a big change. The only real standout clothes I'd worn before were ironic (the gawky plastic glasses frames I wore when I played JV basketball) or legitimately hideous (the baggy green sweater I wore through high school and into college that various girlfriends tried in vain to get me to throw out). Thinking about my shoes made me think more about the rest of my clothes. I started wearing what one might call *outfits*. I was not, as I feared I might be, ridiculed by teenagers in the streets. Admittedly, though, I do benefit from working in a field where casual shoes are the norm, and I'm being graded on the Jewish-guy curve that allowed Jerry Seinfeld to become a low-key sneaker icon.

I also developed what you could consider taste. It wasn't *good* taste necessarily, but it was mine. I prefer shoes with at least a pop of bright, audacious color. I am aware that sometimes I'll purchase high-tops, even though I know that I don't love the feeling of the tongues hugging my lower shins, so I'll lace them up three times a year, maximum. Most days I opt for a pair of low-cut Adidas running shoes, preferably the kind with the upper part made from a knit, sock-like material. I like the style, but also they're incredibly easy to put on, and it feels like wearing slippers outside, which I recommend.

I also started purchasing sneakers as gifts for my loved ones. A pair of sneakers is a great gift[4] for people who think of tennis shoes as the least important items in their footwear rotation. You

---

4   Although it's tough to surprise people with sneakers because you have to first surreptitiously figure out their shoe size.

can show them a whole new world (again, from the ankles down). For my mom's *cough*-th birthday, I bought her a pair of my favorite Adidas runners. She liked them so much that she made a bunch of her mom friends try them on, and they bought pairs of their own, which is very precious, and makes me feel like I made a good choice. When my sister won an award at her hospital the same month I won an Emmy,[5] I bought matching pairs of gold Air Force 1s for the two of us. When I wear mine (which is rare because they are *incredibly* gaudy, even by my tacky standards) I feel proud of her, too.[6]

But in addition to the celebratory and gifted purchases, I also started buying shoes for no good reason at all. I picked up a pair of mismatched Kyrie 4 high-tops for my thirty-third birthday, which was, like every nondecade birthday after age twenty-one, a nonevent. I ordered myself a pair of rare Nike Air Max 1s because it was my wife's birthday (and I was drunk). I bought a pair of Adidas running shoes that say BOSTON SUPER on the side because . . . well, I just wanted them.

By any objective measure, I now own too many pairs of sneakers. It's not like they're made under especially ethical conditions, even after the big sweatshop backlash of the 1990s. More immediately, the space my ever-expanding collection takes up in our apartment is excessive and has required an evolving storage setup

---

5   That's a non-humblebrag. It's very exciting to win an Emmy! If you can swing it, go for it!

6   My dad wears prototypical "dad shoes," white K-Swiss trainers with navy and yellow accents, and is a lost cause.

over the past few years. At first I lined them up in a tidy row between my bedside table and the closet. Soon, though, the row became unwieldy; it started to look as if a basketball team had arranged themselves for a photograph only to be raptured out of their shoes. So I upgraded to a little rack, enough to hold ten or twelve pairs. And then when that became insufficient, I bought two dozen stackable clear plastic cubes, each with a door on the front that allows you to remove a pair of shoes without disturbing the stack.

The cubes worked well for a while, but now I have more sneakers than cubes, and so on top of the stacks are additional stacks of cardboard shoeboxes, ascending to a height that borders on precarious. A few prized pairs sit atop the cardboard boxes. Some others clutter the floor nearby.

I'm afraid to count, but I must have between thirty-five and forty pairs at this point. My habit isn't ruining my life, and I'm definitely not the most frequent or compulsive collector that I know. And no, it is not lost on me that that's exactly what an alcoholic would say in defense of his alcoholism. ("Josh, we need to talk," I imagine my friends sitting down to tell me. "Your ballin' out of control has gotten, well, out of control.")

When I come home late from a stand-up show, I'll leave the lights off as I navigate to my side of the bed on the far end of the room so I don't wake up my wife. I know, I know. Not all heroes wear capes. Sometimes, as I tiptoe through the dark, I will step on a stray sneaker. My ankle will buckle and I'll bang my shin on my bed frame.

Ouch! Shit! I'll think. *My life is pretty good.*

Bizzy

I wasn't quite ready to have a dog, and neither was my wife, but we adopted one anyway, which normally isn't how that works. A dog isn't like a mouse or a baby; you rarely wind up with one living in your house by accident. What happened was, I had promised my then-girlfriend Maris I'd get her a dog when we moved in together. I'd actually promised her a dog as a gift *before* we worked out the details of our impending cohabitation, but she decided her previous apartment, a quirky one-bedroom in Greenpoint, Brooklyn, that she called "Elf House," was too cramped to share with a pet. The dog search, we decided, would wait until we had moved into our new apartment.

This wrinkle in the plan made me a little uneasy. The timing of my original offer was meant to fulfill Maris's long-standing and oft-stated desire for a dog while making it clear that it was *her* dog. I didn't even live in the apartment. How could the dog belong to me? By forestalling the acquisition until we shared a home, though, any pet would definitely be *our* dog. And I didn't know if I was up to the task.

Moving in together felt like enough of a change to take on without introducing a new species into our relationship. I worried that if we got a dog right away, I might conflate the dog-related stress with the move itself, and that I'd feel like we'd rushed into living together. Having a pet felt the same to me as astrological charts: other people love them, and I understand the appeal, but I'd never felt compelled to modify my own lifestyle to accommodate one. Also, much like inviting an animal to live in your home, diving into astrology is an efficient way to give your life over to a force you can never fully understand or control.

And the one pet I did have extensive experience with had not given me a favorable impression of animal companionship.

Until I was about four years old, my family had a cat named Barney. "Had" might even be a generous term for our relationship. It was more like we were haunted by a living creature. Barney stalked our home, vomiting in shoes and on bedsheets. In his late life, he often got stuck on a single step between rooms, front paws on the stair, back paws on the floor. In these instances, he would moan like Robert Plant screeching the bridge of a Led Zeppelin song until one of my parents helped him the rest of the way down. Once, I tried to pick him up around the middle to make the groaning stop. My father quickly stepped in and warned me against trying to heft the cranky tangle of bones and fur.

And, moreover, he cautioned me against petting the cat at all. Barney tended to lash out with his claws when touched for any reason. Years later, a friend of the family told me that my dad used to refer to the cat as "UPS" because he didn't want to call him "Useless Piece of Shit" in front of me and my sister. When the vet finally put Barney to sleep at age eighteen, it wasn't euthanasia, it was an exorcism. My mom will hate that last sentence, but I stand by it.

The idea of bringing a pet into my own life stressed me out. What if we ended up with the dog equivalent of Barney? Stephen King wrote novels about such scenarios. But Maris really wanted a dog. So to prove to her—and to myself—that I was a good and committed partner, I brought up the idea of getting a dog *all the time*.

"The apartment is starting to come together enough it might be ready for a dog soon," I'd offer, after we figured out the perfect spot for the couches we inherited from my grandmother.

"Ooo, there's a dog adoption fair in Union Square," I'd say, noticing a friend's post on Instagram.

"Ahh, a dog, like we will soon have, whenever you say the word, my love," I'd proclaim when a pet food ad showed up on TV.

Maris, reasonably assuming that I must have wanted a pet with every cell in my body, since I was talking about it so damn much, began to browse listings online. She started with Petfinder, which is basically Tinder for pets.[1] She browsed the Petfinder website at work, sending me listings for her favorite dogs. She perused it while we watched TV. We scrolled idly through the app when we were lying in bed at night.

Thanks to the app's search functions, we could seek out exactly the pet we wanted: one to two years old, pug or shih tzu mix,

---

1   I should clarify, it's an app in which you scroll through adoptable animals, not a way for domesticated critters to find each other for "just something casual, let's see how it goes, not looking for anything serious right now lol."

sleepy disposition, good with people. But most of the available dogs fell well outside our parameters. All the good ones, as they say, are either taken or pit bulls. I am not anti–pit bull, but we lived in a seven-hundred-square-foot apartment and both worked full time, leaving us unable to give a large dog the daily SoulCycle class's worth of exercise it would have required. Our lifestyle necessitated a pet with the energy level of yogurt: technically alive, but not especially vigorous. Unfortunately, because every New York City apartment is so cramped you'd expect David Blaine to escape from it as a stunt, small, inert dogs are in high demand. We eventually found the dog of our dreams, but it turned out that a lot of people in New York have the same dream dog.

Much like nuclear proliferation, any search for a dog continues escalating until it reaches its natural conclusion. After Petfinder failed us, Maris moved on to combing the websites of individual shelters. Every few days, she would fall in love with a new dog, all of them pug, shih tzu, and Havanese mixes with names like Ewok and Bartleby. Each dog, I'd have to admit, looked very cute and friendly, an enticing addition to our household. Maris churned out application after application and received rejection after rejection, explaining that the shelter appreciated her interest in adopting Marbles the chug or Bella the Pom-tzu-nese, but alas, one hundred–plus other people shared her enthusiasm, so the pairing was not to be.

After weeks of disappointment, a shelter took pity on Maris and moved her application for a ball of fluff named Gus Gus to the next phase. Since the shelter trying to place Gus Gus was too far away to make a home visit and inspect our apartment up close, they scheduled a sixty-minute phone interview, to make sure we were ready to be adoptive dog parents.

Sixty minutes. On the phone. Talking about a dog. What do you say for an hour about a dog you've never even met before? "We promise we'll feed him and walk him and never dress him in any especially humiliating Halloween costumes for our own amusement"? The shelter also made it clear that we were granted the interview because of Maris's acquaintanceship with Mr. Frito, a French bulldog they had placed with a friend of Maris's in the past. Our adoption liaison described Mr. Frito as "the worst dog they'd ever had" thanks to a combination of physical ailments and personality tics that lent him the bearing of an inbred seventeenth-century Spanish king. He was adorable, but he could barely walk and for much of his life required a diaper, which is a description that you usually anticipate your loved ones growing out of, or dread their growing into. If we had met Mr. Frito and still wanted to adopt, the shelter surmised, we must be decent people.

Still, Maris had been burned too many times and worried about the psychic toll if Gus Gus didn't end up ours after a *sixty-minute phone interview*. So, a few nights before the call, she asked me to post on Twitter about our search and ask for any leads. Maybe someone who followed me on social media knew of a pup who needed a home and didn't require an hour's worth of convincing that we would make capable guardians. I posted a tweet mentioning our desire to adopt a small, smushy-faced dog and inquiring after any leads. Minutes later, an internet acquaintance from Los Angeles replied that a guy she'd met once or twice was looking for a home for a pug that he couldn't take care of.

My acquaintance set us up with her acquaintance and two days later he brought the pug (whom he had been calling Beyoncé, but whose original name had been Suzie) to Brooklyn for us to meet. As soon as they came inside, the dog began wheezing and scrambling in circles. She would pant and stomp for several seconds, and then flop onto her stomach, exhausted, before springing back to her feet.

I fell for her right away.

I loved her squashy little body, like a loaf of white bread with a face smushed onto the front slice and a butt smushed onto the back slice. I was also smitten with her frantic personality. I could tell right away that she was an anxious little weirdo with a lot of baggage—in other words, exactly the kind of traits I gravitate to in a new human or animal friend. Maris often calls me the Kook Whisperer for my ability to remain calm around wacky strangers, relatives, and friends, even in the face of their most unnerving eccentricities. This dog, I knew from the start, was a kook.

We spent a half hour chatting with Mike, the second-degree acquaintance, and as we talked, Beyoncé (née Suzie) grew *slightly* calmer, or I imagined she did. Through our conversation, Maris and I were told the following things about the guy and the dog:

Guy: Moved to New York from LA, where he had worked on the social media for a famous comedian's TV show; was about to go on tour opening for aforementioned famous comedian; just broke up with his girlfriend.

Dog: Six years old, used to live in Vermont with friends of family; couldn't stay with guy, because he already

owned a big dog who liked to play rough; had a crate
but was slightly reluctant to sleep in it.

Nearly all these facts were inaccurate, but we didn't know it
at the time. And why would we have distrusted them? For one
thing, you don't look a gift pug in the mouth. And for another,
who would lie about those kind of details? It turned out, Mike
would, but we wouldn't figure that out for months. Mike left our
apartment with Beyoncé/Suzie, and we promised to be in touch
ASAP with a decision.

"I love her," Maris said as soon as the door closed.

"I love her, too," I said.

I texted Mike immediately. We would be thrilled to take
Suzie/Beyoncé off his hands. Maris canceled the call with Mr.
Frito's old shelter. Mike came back two days later with the dog, her
paperwork, and her belongings: a few cans of food, a large wire-
frame crate, some soft toys, and a blanket. Mike's new girlfriend,
Kelly, had come along for the ride. *Way to bounce back from that
breakup, dude,* I thought. Mike refused to take money for the dog,
but we gave him sixty bucks to cover the gas and tolls from the two
trips to Brooklyn, and a bottle of bourbon as a gift. We felt certain
we had made new great friends, and after Mike and Kelly left, we
all followed each other on social media, so we knew it was real.

Maris chased the dog around the apartment, scooping her up
in her arms and rolling her velvety pug ears between her finger-
tips. I watched, beaming. The hugging appeared to soothe the
antsy little dog, but when Maris put her down, she went back to
wheezing and flopping. After a brief discussion, we decided to
change her name once more to Bizzy (in part because her hyper-

ventilating sounded like the beatboxing of the rapper Biz Markie).
It did feel a little rude to rename a middle-aged dog, but she was
ours now, and besides, her new name wasn't even that different,
phonetically speaking, from the old one. By adopting her, Maris
and I were each convinced that we had made the other's dream
come true, and we were both correct.

The first week of dog-having, though, was a constant horror
punctuated by occasional angelic snuggles. Mike had warned us
that Bizzy didn't like sleeping in her crate, but I was unprepared
for the depths of her loathing. When we put her inside, she barked
furiously at the indignation, like the drunken son of a senator being thrown in jail overnight. She refused to stop barking unless we
put her in bed with us, and once we did, she refused to not throw
up on the blankets. Until the early morning, Bizzy circled and
probed the spaces between our feet, her constant wheezing dry
and scratchy like acrylic nails thrumming against a wicker basket.

"If this is what having a pet is like, I don't know if I can do
it," I moaned to Maris (and the heavens) somewhere between one
and two in the morning on the third night. *Maybe we can find
someone else who wants this dog* was the unspoken second half of
that thought.

I'd begun to worry that I didn't have the constitution for pet
ownership, which certainly boded poorly for my potential future
as the parent of a human. You hear all the time about people getting a pet as training for kids. You rarely hear about them then
deciding, *Nope. Never mind*. Not that we had even decided we
wanted children, but other people had started to bring it up, in
part because of how quickly we took on a pet.

When you and your partner get a dog, everyone in your life

takes it as a sign that you're practicing to have kids. Of course, once you're married, people take *everything* as a sign you're about to have kids. Moving into a bigger apartment? Room for a nursery. Going on vacation? A last hurrah before the baby. Buying new pajamas? That's the outfit in which you plan to conceive. With every decision you make, friends and relatives can't wait to read the tea leaves, and it always seems to be You're Having a Baby! brand tea.

But at least, if we had to, we could give the dog away, which is not quite as easy to do with a baby. There is a *lot* of red tape in passing off a human infant, and people ask *questions*.

Maris and I were also starting to have some questions about Bizzy and her curiously no-strings-attached adoption. When we started sifting through her paperwork so we could schedule her an appointment with a local vet, we learned that she wasn't six years old, as Mike had told us; she was actually eight. Two years isn't a *huge* difference, but it was enough that it may have dissuaded us from meeting her in the first place, especially since we'd started off hoping to find a dog between ages one and two. In dog years, the difference between one and eight is the difference between taking in a second-grader and adopting your mom's friend Alice who's almost ready to retire.

But, for someone who had taken in a needy pup on short notice, confusing a six-year-old pug with an eight-year-old one seemed like an understandable error. After all, you can't ask a dog how old she is, nor will she reveal that information with a sassy T-shirt reading FORTY IS THE NEW FLIRTY or PINOT MONEY, PINOT PROBLEMS.

There were other issues with Mike's story, too, though. Soon after we met him, I started poking around online for videos of his comedy or listings for shows he'd performed on. I wanted to learn more about his work so I could help him adjust to the New York City comedy scene. And what came up was . . . nothing. Not a single flyer for a gig at a bar. Not a second of footage of him on-stage. Not one credit on the IMDB page for the show he told us he worked for. Again, though, I could imagine a world in which those omissions made sense. Not every opening act for a big name shows up on a venue's website. And sometimes certain credits fall through the cracks at IMDB.

And yeah, some people, even when they work in entertain-ment, prefer to stay more or less "off the grid." On the other hand, a desire to reduce his digital footprint didn't quite square with the fact that we'd met him online. There was also his constant lurking on Maris's and my social media accounts and rapid comments ("So cute!" "Miss ya, Bizzy!") on any pug-related photos or statuses we posted. But it was precisely the enthusiasm of those comments that kept us from worrying too much. "He's so nice!" we reasoned. "There must be some reasonable explanation for this other stuff."

Meanwhile, Bizzy settled into her new home. As she adjusted, the mist of her anxiety dissipated, and her regular disposition be-gan to reveal itself. Within two weeks, she started sleeping through the night as well as most of the day. Her personality, it turned out, was basically "teddy bear that came *some* of the way to life." She loves to snack and to snuggle, and she gets winded after just a few minutes of exercise. A dog after my own heart. Maybe I'm projecting, or maybe it's just that we were the ones with access to her treats, but it felt like Bizzy started to love us, too.

After her initial period of bed vomiting, Bizzy turned out to be what you might call a Very Good Girl. Most important, she doesn't do the three things you *really* don't want a dog to do (spewing bodily fluids in the house, chewing up your stuff, and biting people). She does have some stubborn habits, though, and like the old dogs you read about, she refuses to break them. She hates the sound of our doorbell, and she barks when she hears other dogs in the hallway. As soon as she sees who it is, though, she calms right down, because she loves anything she can see, and her worst enemy is anyone she can only hear.

Also, after dinner, without fail, Bizzy climbs onto my wife's leg and humps wildly until she gets winded and falls off after seven seconds, like a reverse bull ride. It happens every night. It happens only to my wife, never to me, which makes me feel bad because I'm not the favorite, and then I feel insane for being disappointed that a dog doesn't want to have sex with my leg. Also, while she no longer spends all night rooting around the bed like a truffle pig, Bizzy prefers to sleep between my or my wife's legs through the night, which is more comfortable for the twenty-four-pound dog than the person-size person who has to contort around her. But I don't care that much, because she's so cute I could die.

Since Bizzy didn't require housebreaking or leash training, taking her in felt less like having a baby and more like taking on a new roommate. We were never on high alert that she would pee on our shoes, but we did have to become attuned to the times of day she expected to go out. Bizzy has preferences and predilections, and by choosing to have her in our life, we had to accept her as she is. If we wanted her (and we did!), we had to accept the occasional hypervigilant barking and the separation anxiety and leg sex.

It's the same as when you meet human adults. It's helpful to admit that you're not going to change who they are. Sure, they may adjust to you a little, but at some point you have to decide whether you're going to let them sleep between your knees (metaphorically speaking, usually) because that's just what they do. Instead of assuming what others want, you have to really listen to them and give them what they actually need. Once Bizzy became less of a yapping, puking terror and more of a sweet old lady who ate off my floor, I felt more Zen about the whole experience.

A few weeks into our relationship's BC (Bizzy centric) era, Maris got a text from a friend named (let's say) Carly, asking if we knew a guy named (let's say) Mike Lastname. She replied that we did, and in fact he was a very nice guy who'd given us a dog for free. Carly's reply:

> Oh, I met him at a bar, and he told me he used to date my friend and that he wrote a bunch of songs for her band. But I texted her and she said that they never dated, and he was just an acquaintance who watched her big dog while her band went on tour.

In retrospect, that should have told us anything we needed to know about Mike, but his weird behavior seemed like an aberration rather than a pattern. After all, he had given us a dog for free. A dog who, by this time, no longer reacted to every noise in the hallway by barking like she was doing background vocals on a DMX song. We tried to give Mike the benefit of the doubt. Maybe, we thought, he was just insecure about his accomplishments after moving to a new city, so he embellished his professional connections. Everyone has lied on a résumé, right? Well, he was just showing that punched-up résumé to people outside his professional sphere. Yes, looking back, I know how ridiculous that sounds.

That was not the last we heard of Mike. He continued to leave messages on Instagram and Facebook by pictures of Biz ("Those jowls!" "What a queen!"). He showed up at one of my stand-up shows and chatted up other friends in the crowd. He seemed, to our faces and on our feeds, like a sweet and charming dude.

But then another female friend reached out, over a Twitter direct message:

> Hey? Do you know Mike Lastname?

This time I was more wary.

> A little. We got our dog from him, but we're not close. Why do you ask?

I dreaded her response. My friend wrote back,

> I met him at a bar, and he told me he was working on a TV pilot with Well-Known but Not Household Name Famous TV Writer Woman. I know her a little

bit and asked her about it, and she'd never heard
of him.

Shit. If we didn't before, we now definitely had both enough information and enough distance to relax our gaze and let the real picture of Mike Lastname emerge from the Magic Eye poster of his lies. All his flimsy show business stories shared a common trait: they were both impressive and incredibly hard to verify. The fake jobs he bragged about were always the kind that were hard to cross-check against the credits of a TV show or on the internet. Unfortunately for him, he kept lying to people who had legitimate connections to the world he pretended to inhabit.

Who knows how many other people he told that he was a personal assistant to Chris Rock or a dialect coach for Dwayne "the Rock" Johnson and never bothered to vet his story. I don't know why he was doing it. Maybe to convince people to have sex with him. Definitely that was the reason, right? But why was he lying to us, too? Had he been trying to arrange a foursome with me, Maris, and Kelly? There have to be easier ways to do that than acquiring and giving away a pug. Plus he made up the fact that he owned a dog of his own, which is a true sociopath move. That's basically the way you make the audience sympathize with an unlikable movie character. "Oh sure, he's a hit man. But he loves that dog so much." THAT IS LITERALLY THE PREMISE OF THE MOVIE *JOHN WICK*.

By the time Kelly (who Maris and I knew had dated Mike because we met her UNLESS SHE WAS A PAID ACTRESS OR A CYBORG, WHICH AT THIS POINT WAS NOT OFF THE

TABLE) wrote to tell us that Mike was a "toxic" person whom we should "beware" of and that she had "cut him out of her life," we thanked her for her insight, but we weren't *surprised*. We didn't know anything about Mike that seemed sinister enough to make a public scene, but we quietly unfriended him on Facebook and unfollowed him on Instagram.

A few more months passed, and we didn't hear about Mike much at all. Bizzy had become such a part of our lives that she didn't even remind us of him anymore. She was ours, through and through. And then one night Mike flew too close to the sun. Apparently he had been out at a bar again, lying about punching up jokes for a show starring an Actually Famous Actress, who was alerted to his untruths and did not take kindly to them. I know that because a couple of days later, my various online newsfeeds were full of headlines like "Actually Famous Actress Rips into Liar for Pretending to Work on Her Show." Even before I read the article, my first thought was, *Hey! I know that guy!* Actually Famous Actress had not let the résumé embellishing slide the way other people had in the past, and she called him out onstage by name during a live performance she was doing.

"That's so weird," Maris said after I forwarded her one of the many articles outing Mike Lastname as a dirtbag. "I had seen a picture of him with Actually Famous Actress on his Instagram. I assumed they were real-life friends." It hit us both together. Mike hadn't been trying to recruit us for an orgy. We were his alibi. Our correspondence was designed to make him seem legitimate to outsiders. All the clues were right there in front of us. I wish I had been holding a coffee cup with Mike's name on it that I could have dropped and watched shatter in slow motion. We immediately called up his Instagram profile to see who else he'd been using for sinister gains, but he had deleted all of his social media accounts. Just like that, he was gone.[2]

Of all the deceit, misinformation, and misunderstanding that happened over the course of Bizzy's adoption, one moment stung the most. As it became clear that Mike had misled us on just about every detail he'd offered, we figured out that he was (at best) a pathological liar. But there was one thing we couldn't get over: Who lies about having a dog? Maris couldn't shake the fear that because of Mike's deception, *we* had somehow come into possession of a stolen pug.[3] Under any other circumstances, I would have immediately written off the theory that someone had stolen an elderly dog, brought it across state lines, and given it away to strangers for free. But in this case, we had to at least *entertain* the idea. After all, the rest of Mike's backstory had been a sham; maybe Bizzy's was, too. Maybe there were no elderly friends of the family in Vermont who went into assisted living, as Mike had told us. Maybe he'd seen a pug in the window of a pet store in Queens, smashed the glass, scooped the dog up, and unloaded her on a couple of saps, just to feel alive.

Maris did a quick series of Google searches ("stolen + pug," "stolen + pug + Vermont," "stolen + pug + elderly," etc.), which turned up no incriminating results. If Bizzy was dognapped, it had

---

2   That's a line from *The Usual Suspects*, a movie in which the real-life monster Kevin Spacey plays a fictional monster named Keyser Söze.

3   A "hot" dog, if you will. And if you won't, good choice. I respect that.

gone unreported. On the other hand, lots of crime victims never go to the police. Maybe there was some element of blackmail involved. Maybe Bizzy's old family consisted of undocumented immigrants who didn't trust law enforcement. Our capacity for conspiracy theory by this point was off the charts.

In a final effort to learn the truth, I shuffled through Bizzy's paperwork and called a number I found on a scrap of paper.

"Hello?" answered the voice of an older woman.

"Hi. I'm Josh. I have a pug named Bizzy, but maybe she used to belong to you or someone you know. Her name may have been Suzie back then. Mike gave her to us. We just wanted to make sure that no one else had a rightful claim to the dog."

Silence. I realized that if I wasn't talking to the right person, what I had just said must have sounded like the ramblings of a truly deranged weirdo. Finally she replied.

"Oh. Huh. Yeah, nobody wants that dog."

I still don't know who was on the other end of the line. She may have been Bizzy's previous owner. She could have been the next of kin. Maybe she was just Mike, wearing a wig and doing an old lady voice. I'm not sure why, but I imagine if he was doing the voice, he'd be wearing a wig. Whoever she was, she was wrong. Because Maris really wanted that dog, and finally, I did, too.

One night at a comedy show six months later, I ran into Actually Famous Actress. I was drunk, and Also Famous Comedian Friend convinced me to tell her all about Bizzy and our strange connection. Actually Famous Actress, a stranger, did not have any interest in hearing about my dog. So in that way, it was like having a kid after all.

A Partial List of Names I Call My Dog, Whose Real Name Is Bizzy

Biz
Bizzy
Bizzy Bee
Bizzy Bean
Business
Lil' Business
Lil' Miss
Bunny
Bunches
Bunz
Bunzo
Bunzou
Bunzadonna
Bunzadella
Bunzadelia
Sweet Pea
Fatso

Flatso (when she lies down flat on the ground)

Flopsy

Sass Monster

Munchkin

Goob

Goober

Pudge

Smush

Smushington

Monster

Gremlin

Goblin

Mrs. Velvet Ears

"I Also Do Michael Jackson"

"So," said Bengey (or, as we knew him now, "DJ Bengey") as he leaned forward from his perch on the love seat in our living room, "in addition to my DJ services . . . I also do Michael Jackson. Would you like me to do that at the wedding?"

I wasn't sure what he meant, precisely. To be diplomatic, it's fair to say the youngest member of the Jackson 5 was known for several different things. Was Bengey offering to use our wedding reception as a venue for turning a backyard into an amusement park? Bringing zombies back to life? Or, perhaps most improbably and inappropriately, winning a posthumous lifetime achievement Grammy Award? It's not *your* day, dude. Then there were the issues of MJ's—let's say, diplomatically again—unorthodox childcare strategy. I figured that was not what he was proposing. But I didn't know exactly what was at stake for my wedding day, and I didn't ask.

"Sure!" I said. "That sounds really cool!"

Bengey had been having a tough time. He moonlit[1] as a

---

1   Or, if it's during the day, do you say *sunlit*?

professional dog walker in north Brooklyn, which was the capacity in which we met him, but his real passion was music. When Union Hall, a beloved local venue, shut down for several months after a fire,[2] Bengey's most reliable DJ gig dried up, leaving him scrambling for work. When Maris and I came home from work one day to a note on our kitchen counter asking if we knew of anyone with the need for a disc jockey in the near future, we hired him right away to do our wedding. Sure, we didn't know him as well as Bizzy, our fat pug who spent forty-five minutes with him three days a week while Maris and I were at work. But how well do you know any DJ, really?

And yes, that sounds like a metaphysical question (What *is* a DJ? How can one know if one truly possesses DJ qualities?) but is really very practical. The DJ is the person you know the least who has the biggest influence on your wedding reception—I mean, unless the caterer decides to poison you. But Bengey seemed nice. Bizzy liked him, after all, which we knew because she occasionally refused to poop for substitute walkers and always pooped when Bengey took her out. That is a high compliment coming from a dog.

Any friend of Bizzy's was a friend of ours, we figured. Usually that statement is literal. She doesn't go out on her own much, because she's one foot tall and doesn't have thumbs, and she pretty much knows only the people we introduce her to. We were glad to hire Bengey to help fill his calendar and also check one more item

---

2   Nobody was hurt, in case you were worried!

off our Sisyphean wedding prep to-do list. And look, once you've committed to doing someone that kind of favor, why not give him the green light to "do Michael Jackson" as well?

"Great," Bengey said. "I've got an outfit, and I'm also a dancer."

"Oh, okay," Maris added. "One song seems like it could be fun I guess. Maybe 'The Way You Make Me Feel.' It's already on our playlist."

Making the playlist was literally the first wedding planning we'd done. Technically, two playlists. A sixty-minute compilation for the preceremony "cocktail hour," and 180+ minutes for the reception itself. We compiled it while on a road trip a week after we got engaged. We were very excited about the playlist, and when Maris invoked it, I remembered that the wedding was Her Special Day as well as mine, and it would be rude to impose unwanted dance performances on her. After all, I was marrying Maris, not DJ Bengey.

"Yeah," I reiterated. "That sounds good. It is already on the playlist."

"Great," Bengey replied.

We all stood up, including Bizzy, who hopped off the couch, ready to be walked, confused that the three of us had been talking together so long, not walking her. Maris and I shook Bengey's hand, and I didn't think about Michael Jackson until the day of our wedding. And even then, the concept of our wedding DJ impersonating the late King of Pop at the reception merely flickered across my consciousness, an abstraction more than a reality.

I had other things on my mind that day. I wasn't *nervous*, just *busy*. There was family to wrangle. There were pictures to take. I had to remember to bring my change of shoes to the venue.

There's no real reason to be afraid on your wedding day. Even if everything goes wrong with the logistics, it'll be fine. You'll still end up married. And as long as you don't leave in the middle, *you* aren't going to ruin the event. No matter what you do, half of the people in the room are there explicitly to support you. You could cry, stammer, trip, or punch someone in the back of the head, and at worst, you'd lose 50 percent of the crowd. It's *your* wedding, and a general rule of public speaking is even more true on that day: everyone is rooting for you, and nobody is going to be mad if you screw up a little bit.

The only legitimate wedding-day fear is that your partner will get cold feet and bail. And if you have any inkling that could happen, *holy shit, you two shouldn't be getting married in the first place.*

I'm not exactly an unbiased source, but in my opinion, Maris and I had a very good wedding. Some of that comes down to good luck: The weather held out. There was no family drama. No one "spoke now or forever held their peace." But in my (again, biased) view, we also did a good job with the planning.

If you are wondering how to make a wedding excellent, here are a few tips:

- No bridesmaids or groomsmen.
  You're trying to celebrate your love, not rank your closest friends and send them on a yearlong scavenger hunt for matching outfits and accessories (or two scavenger hunts if the bachelor or bachelorette party involves a planned scavenger hunt).

- Plenty of chairs, but no assigned seating.

  People decide who they want to sit next to every day of their lives. They can also do it at your wedding. If there's friction between relatives, they can suck it up for three hours. This also enables superior, buffet-style dining, so no guest has to passive-aggressively be like, "Hey, not to be a pain in the ass, but . . . I'm pretty sure I asked for the fish. No big deal, but I haven't eaten red meat in eleven years, so there's no way I would have chosen the steak. Just wondering if maybe somebody else got the fish that I absolutely, definitely ordered. No presh."

- Limit the speeches.

  We let only our parents talk. Well, everyone could talk, but no one else was given a microphone and the room's full attention. If a friend wanted to say a few meaningful words, he or she could quit being a coward and say them to my face.

And if you really want to make your event memorable, hire a Michael Jackson impersonator and fail to consider the practical ramifications of that decision for several weeks. Sure, this offhand gesture of goodwill toward an acquaintance could become legitimately uncomfortable. But, in my experience, it led to the second-best moment of my wedding day.

(The best moment is not a great story. It was the quiet instant right after the ceremony when everything was in transition, and

Maris and I had a moment to ourselves to find an out-of-the-way place to check in with one another and be in love. That is not a euphemism, I swear.)

Through the ceremony and cocktail hour, DJ Bengey performed admirably, hitting all the right cues, and even turning the music down a little bit when my dad thought it was too loud. He stuck mostly to the list of songs we'd given him, although he did defy Maris's "No line dances!" direction, much to her dismay but the extreme delight of my aunt Judith, who had been waiting all evening to show off her Cha Cha Slide and Macarena skills.

Then, about halfway through the reception, the music stopped. DJ Bengey stepped out from behind the table that held his equipment. He had peeled off his suit jacket and replaced it with a red leather bomber. He held a microphone in one hand. The other was sheathed in a rhinestone-studded glove. He was, of course, doing Michael Jackson.

"Ladies and gentlemen," he announced. "I have a surprise for the bride and the groom. I told them about this a few weeks ago, but I'm pretty sure they've forgotten by now."

While this performance was not exactly top of mind for me, I had *absolutely not* forgotten about that conversation. When someone tells you that he intends to impersonate Michael Jackson at your wedding, it tends to stick with you. But while I remembered that Bengey's performance loomed, I hadn't told anyone else about it.

So when he emerged in costume, it was a surprise for everyone *except* me and Maris. And, given Bengey's intro, our guests had no reason to believe that we weren't also stunned by this turn of events. Some relatives who had not noted what the DJ looked like earlier were not even aware that's who Bengey was. They assumed an intoxicated friend had hijacked the sound system for an impromptu toast.

"Hit it!" said DJ Bengey to my friend Will, whom he had deputized as assistant DJ for this crucial moment. Will hit it. The opening snare drum from "Billie Jean" blared over the sound system, full blast. "Billie Jean," if you remember, was not the Michael Jackson song we had put on our playlist. It is also not a good song for weddings, period. If you aren't familiar, it's basically a five-minute-long recounting of a paternity suit. The music choice felt, let's say, inauspicious for day one of a new marriage.

But there was no time to quibble or protest. Bengey retrieved two Party City–type plastic fedoras from the DJ table. He placed one on my head and one on Maris's. By the time the signature *bloop bloops* of the song had kicked in, a circle had formed around DJ Bengey. Some of the party guests clapped their hands to the beat in delight. Others peered at the spectacle before them, not quite sure what was happening. A sense of intrigue filled the room like the synthetic cloud made by a fog machine.[3]

To his credit, DJ Bengey had some excellent moves. His hand motions were crisp. His footwork was fluid. He even pulled off a credible moonwalk. By the second chorus, he had brought the whole crowd onto his side with his skills, despite not looking a lot

---

3   It's worth noting that this happened before a recent HBO documentary foregrounded the reasons that Michael Jackson's music might not feel good for everyone to hear, and the mood at the wedding remained upbeat.

like Michael Jackson. He's Black, yes, but also he's at least 6'2"
and has dreadlocks. Through all of MJ's numerous style choices
through the years, he was never 6'2" with dreadlocks. But despite
that discrepancy, DJ Bengey managed to evoke vintage Michael
Jackson even to the 20 percent of the audience composed of old
Jewish cousins who pictured late-period surgical mask Mike more
readily than *Thriller* Mike.

Here's the best part, though. The song's outro began. In case
you don't remember, "Billie Jean" takes roughly as long to ease
into its conclusion as a flight after the pilot announces the final
descent. ("Another *thirty minutes* of this? Really?") In the wan-
ing minutes of "Billie Jean," Bengey danced back toward me and
Maris. With a practiced flick of his wrist, he plucked the plastic
hat from my head. He leaned toward me and stage-whispered
"The hat lights up" over MJ's pleading vocals and of course the
ongoing synthesizer *bloops*. I think he even winked, but I may be
remembering that wrong.

My closest friends and relatives as well as Maris's closest friends
and relatives stood in a circle around us. After all, it was our wedding, and we were talking to a man dressed as, and dancing in the
style of, Michael Jackson. They furrowed their brows, not having
heard Bengey's promise, and watched as he hit the little button on
the inside of the hat four . . . five . . . six times.

The hat did not light up.

Cool as a beer in the back of the fridge, DJ Bengey dropped
the hat back onto my head. He leaned in to whisper again: "The
hat used to light up."

He shrugged and moonwalked across the room while I doubled over, fully overwhelmed by the moment, my head buried in my hands, my eyes streaming with laugh tears. And when I told Maris what he'd said, she laughed, too.

I guess what I'm saying is sometimes things work out for the best.[4]

---

4   Also, if you were at my wedding, and I didn't get to talk to you after Bengey's performance . . . that's what happened.

The Best Moments of My Wedding #3–10

3. Hearing my wife's vows

4. Reading my wife my vows

5. Seeing so many friends and relatives together in one room

6. The custom T-shirt my dad made with the punch line to one of my stand-up jokes about him on it that he changed into before giving a toast

7. The presence of cake[1]

8. Maris's four-year-old niece's incredibly vigorous dancing

9. Changing into sneakers after the ceremony

10. Lin-Manuel Miranda writing us personalized song lyrics about getting married on Twitter

---

1   Our caterer called us the night before the wedding and said, "You guys don't want cake, right?" And we were like, "Yes, of course we want cake. We came to your office and tasted one cake and knew that it was the one we wanted because it had the most chocolate in it." Maris has diabetes, and she eats a big dessert only three or four times a year, usually on special occasions. There is, on these nights, joy in her eyes that can verge on teary. My favorite thing in the whole world is to watch Maris eat cake.

Don't Let the Bastards Grind You Down

For the last four years I have couched every admission that my personal life and career have trended in a positive direction with a caveat about the state of the world at large.

"I'm doing great other than how terrible things are," I'd say. Or, "Everything's been really good except for . . . you know . . . everything."

The assault on civil liberties, reproductive health, and the social safety net has made increasing progress thanks to the relentlessness of its perpetrators and the colossal shithead charisma of an American president who makes people the world over shake their heads and mutter, *"This* fuckin' guy?" But things haven't just gotten bad recently. For a lot of people, things *already were* bad.

The realization manifested in different ways for everyone. Some of my friends, disillusioned with electoral politics, threw themselves into grassroots organizing. Others, determined to change the system from within, ran for office. A few simply followed the president on social media and moaned in anguish at each incoherent post. I struggled to define a line between activism and obsession, and on the other end of the "how much to engage" spectrum, self-preservation and cowardice.

I imagine that if you have made it this far into this book without throwing it into a fire or sending me an angry/concerned email, you may have wrestled with similar questions. It's hard to know how to look out for people, and how much to give of yourself. What constitutes giving too much, and, on the other hand, what's stopping you from giving more?

I attended the first Women's March in New York City in January 2017 and the second one a year later.[1] The first year, my wife, Maris, made a sign reading: NOLITE TE BASTARDES CARBORUNDORUM! an almost-Latin phrase taken from Margaret Atwood's novel *The Handmaid's Tale* that means, roughly, "Don't let the bastards grind you down!" Maris and I met up with friends in Midtown Manhattan for the protest. We trudged through the crowded city streets, energized by fear and outrage and thwarted by the slow progress of the marchers in front of us. It took almost two hours, but we walked the twentysomething blocks from Grand Central Terminal up to Trump Tower. We booed, gave the building the middle finger, and then headed home, unsure of precisely what to do next.

There was a real emotional power to coming together in support of a common cause, and in this case the cause was "the rights of 50ish percent of the world's population." There were signs promoting abortion rights, demanding an end to the gender (and racial) pay gap, decrying sexual harassment and assault, and calling for equal rights for transgender women. Even if you are the kind of

---

1   I missed the third march because I was traveling for work.

person who does not think those are all worthy goals (and they are, by the way), you would have to be a real asshole to oppose an event with the blanket goal of *improving the lives of women.*

Maris and I lasted only half an hour at the second Women's March, in part because it *started* at the foot of a Trump-branded property by Columbus Circle on Fifty-Ninth Street. When you get to give a Donald Trump–adjacent building the middle finger at the beginning of a protest, there's nowhere to go from there but down. We shuffled five blocks north in thirty minutes and then, not knowing what we were walking toward, we wriggled past the metal crowd control barriers and doubled back the way we came. We felt guilty, but nobody would miss us, we reasoned.

It's easy to support the kind of protests whose goals even the most ardent and disingenuous opponents have a hard time willfully misconstruing. The ones that are planned months in advance for a Saturday afternoon. Where parents bring kids with hand-knit hats and cute puns written in glitter to protest gender inequality. In New York City, it's not exactly a controversial stance, even in Midtown Manhattan at the foot of a towering building bearing the Trump name.

My record is spottier in terms of showing up for more difficult demonstrations. The ones called for at the last minute to protest a new flare-up of an old injustice, a cold sore on the lip of liberty. When, say, a man selling loose cigarettes is choked to death by a police officer and a vigil is planned. Or when a few hundred people barricade an ICE facility, using their bodies as a barrier between undocumented immigrants and incarceration. In those cases, it's easy to *not* show up, because I am scared of the fight.

When President Trump implemented his original ban against

travelers from several majority-Muslim nations into the United States, people mobilized hard and fast. Crowds assembled outside airport terminals. Makeshift legal clinics sprouted up in waiting areas to help reunite people with family members, including some who were literally in the sky as the order was handed down. The administration hadn't considered these issues, or, more likely, did not give a shit what became of these people.

I missed the first round of protests, ironically because I was already at JFK airport in Queens, waiting to board a cross-country flight. It felt like riding out an entire hurricane in the eye. *Wow, it sure looks turbulent right outside, but weirdly I'm untouched.* While I sat in the terminal, I donated some money to some refugee assistance organizations and read the news on my phone until the battery nearly flatlined.

When I tour as a comedian, I usually set up a merch table after the shows and donate the profits to a good cause, an LGBT youth crisis hotline or hurricane relief in Puerto Rico, and then I personally match the donations. And sure, that's nice. But also it gets my albums and posters and pins into people's hands. So how nice is it, really?

I never quite measure up to the person I'd like to be. My contributions to causes come from a distance. I try to use my modest platform to disseminate useful information or raise funds, but I am trying to do more, especially in light of the fact that my straight white male privilege shields me from many of the uglier abuses faced by women, people of color, and queer people (not to mention those whose identities involve an intersection of those qualities).

Wouldn't it be better if I were an immigration lawyer or a labor organizer or a tenants' rights advocate or a special education

teacher like my friends from college? Or maybe this is the best way
to support the good work being done by people in those fields. Or
maybe *that* is just something people who don't want to try harder
say to avoid having to try harder. It's hard to know what the right
way is to do the right thing.

Meanwhile, on Election Day 2016, I was too intimidated by
the phone-banking website and the prospect of being hung up on
by strangers to actually sign up to make calls on Hillary Clinton's
behalf. Say what you will about Hillary Clinton—not to me; whisper it into a paper bag and then throw the bag in a fire, because I
do not want to talk about her with you—but by November 8, 2016,
she was the better and only choice for president, and I did not help
because why? I didn't wanna sign up for an email list?

Around the same time as the airport protests over the travel
ban, the news was interviewing a white supremacist—because they
do that now—and then someone ran by and punched him in the
face. And it was awesome. I watched the footage, on loop, a lot. I
can say with confidence that it was as good as any of the Captain
America movies, even though I have never seen them.

Seeing an avowed white nationalist get punched in the head
by a concerned citizen felt as good to me as I imagine it felt bad to
him. Some people wrote essays about how we should not celebrate
the punching of a Nazi, how it is a slippery slope, and who is to
say who is and is not a Nazi? "Is anyone with 'unorthodox views'
or 'unpopular opinions' all of a sudden a Nazi?" they asked. The
answer to that question is "Of course not." First of all, racism is as-
tonishingly orthodox and popular in the present day. Second, you
have to draw the line over who's good to punch somewhere, and at

least a segment of that line should point at anyone who says white people are intrinsically superior to people of other races.

Even though I don't support all, or even most punching, I come down squarely on the side of people who punch Nazis, simply because it rules when bad things happen to white supremacists. It's a moral good, and I bet it feels amazing to do. I'll take it this far: I'd like to think that I'm the kind of guy who would, himself, punch a Nazi in the face. But I worry that I don't have it in me. Or that I wouldn't do a good job at punching. Or that I'd accidentally punch a non-Nazi with that swooping haircut they have now and then I'd have to be like, "Whoops, sorry, Macklemore!"

It's *good* to read the news and donate to charity and vote, but it's not *brave*, and it's not even really a sacrifice. There's nothing bold about donating money you can afford to part with. There is no risk in a man saying "I support women!" And sure, it's a pain in the ass to stand in line on election day at a local elementary school (the only time you can do that without having kids, by the way) to fulfill the obligation of coloring in a few ovals on a piece of paper. But that is the bare minimum. Instagramming an I VOTED! sticker is like showing off a pin that says I DIDN'T EVADE MY TAXES!

On my way home from San Francisco, I once again wound up at JFK during the same round of travel ban protests. The demonstrations had dwindled in intensity but were still flickering at the edges of some airport terminals, and I was determined to find one and join in. Unfortunately, because of the size and complexity of JFK, I could hear the crowd chanting, but after twenty minutes of searching, I couldn't find them.

I went back inside and wandered over to the makeshift law

firm that had taken root near the taxi stand. Everything about the cluster of disheveled professionals was impressive. Many of the lawyers had been there all day, pro bono. They'd generated some kind of ad hoc workflow, and all of them had their heads in a laptop or pressed against a phone, in deep concentration. I marveled at their dedication and the fact that they'd found enough outlets to power their whole ersatz office. I wanted to be helpful, but I am a goober with no practical skills. I have a sub-*SVU* knowledge of the law.

I walked across the atrium to the Dunkin' Donuts Express kiosk, where I purchased a dozen cups of coffee. Again, I was throwing money at the problem, this time from up close. I brought the coffees back to where the lawyers were and approached one who appeared to be doing the triage for incoming crises.

"Do you need any coffee?" I asked.

"Maybe someone does," she said with a shrug, and pointed to a table filled with provisions. Bottles of water, Pepperidge Farm cookies, and Twizzlers. Dry goods purchased from a Hudson News. I put the cups down amid the other supplies.

"I brought some coffee," I said, barely above a whisper, so as not to disturb anyone in the middle of urgent work. Nobody looked, obviously. "Thanks for what you're doing," I mumbled.

I think I did *something*. Maybe one of those cups of coffee found its way into the hands of a lawyer who stayed up an extra hour poring over visas and wrangling vulnerable immigrants away from the TSA. Or maybe all twelve drinks sat on the table until they grew cold and undesirable, and a custodial worker shook his head and dumped them into a trash barrel. Probably it was somewhere in the middle. It never hurts to buy someone a cup of coffee.

I got in a taxi and headed home, the chanting of the protesters outside still audible but invisible.

It's impossible for everyone to be on the front line of every battle, but I'm trying to get there as often as I can. In the meantime, I want to make things as good as I can in my everyday life: sparing a few dollars for a person in need, stepping in when I hear someone say something cruel or bigoted, celebrating and supporting art made by people of color, eating vegan meals at least *sometimes*, treating the people around me well, listening to their needs, and attempting to improve over time rather than retreating into a comfortable privilege cocoon. And that especially applies when the injustice in question doesn't touch my life directly.

There's a quote often attributed to activist Angela Davis: "In a racist society, it's not enough to be non-racist—you have to be anti-racist." I apologize to Dr. Davis if she didn't actually say that, but it's a really good quote, so I don't apologize that much. Regardless of who said it, it's a clarifying perspective, and in keeping with that doctrine, I'm working on being less "not bad" and more "actively good," in both big and small ways, even when it's uncomfortable and impolite. One of the best parts of writing this book was considering the precise ways I could be doing more to help instead of fretting about not doing enough. I'm trying, more than ever, not to avoid the ugly aspects of the world, but to look them in the eyes, and occasionally punch them in the face.

Because sometimes the best way to be kind is to not be nice.

About the Author

Josh Gondelman is a comedian and writer and producer for *Desus & Mero* on Showtime. Josh has earned two Peabody Awards, three Emmy Awards, and three WGA Awards for his work on *Last Week Tonight with John Oliver* on HBO. His writing has also appeared in the *New York Times*, *New York* magazine, and *The New Yorker*. He performs stand-up comedy basically wherever. He lives in New York City with his wife and their pug.

Acknowledgments

Thank you to Maris, the smartest and prettiest and most generous person I know, and to Bizzy, our chubby cloud of a dog. Thanks to my mom and dad for their nearly 3.5 decades of unwavering support. To Jenna, my sister, for being an ideal sibling.

To Stephanie Hitchcock, for not being impressed by my bullshit and for using her incredible insight to help make this book as good as it can be, and to everyone at Harper Perennial for getting behind it.

To all my friends and relatives (especially Mom, Dad, and Jenna) who let me use their names or at the very least their likenesses in stories, and also to my grandparents, whose names and likenesses I used without permission. (Thanks! Sorry!)

To everyone who has ever paid me a fair wage to write for them.

Thanks to Noah for helping make me an author as well as a writer. And Chenoa, Taryn, Ayala, Adam, and Josh (different guy), for believing in me and advocating on my behalf.

To anyone who read this book, especially if you got this far. Holy shit that's some dedication.